THE DARK DAD

THE DARK DAD

War and trauma — a daughter's tale

MARY KISLER

This book is dedicated to several groups of people: to the ordinary men who were part of the chaos of the Battle of Sidi Rezegh; to those who gave up their young lives for a cause barely understood; to the men who survived to fight another day; and to those who spent long years as POWs. The body, when wounded, can usually mend over time, but a damaged or broken mind often takes longer. I hope that other people of my generation who experienced childhoods like ours may find some solace in knowing that theirs was not an isolated experience and find the compassion to forgive their fathers when they didn't come up to the mark.

The Dark Dad is also dedicated to my brothers, John and Michael, my childhood partners in crime, whom I love and deeply admire and whose company I have treasured. Sadly, Michael didn't live to see this book published, but in the days before his death we talked a lot about what our family life had been like. I might have said that as a child he was the most anxious of all of us, but he brushed that aside, telling me that once John and I had left home things began to settle, and that he was glad to have had some pleasant years before he, too, flew the nest.

Contents

The painting in the hallway: Johannes Vermeer's *Girl with a Pearl Earring*, which hangs in Mauritshuis, The Hague.

1.

The dark dad

I stand at the doorway, fists clenched, gazing up at the little painting that hangs on the narrow strip of wall above the telephone table. The young woman seems to be glancing in my direction, her hair covered by a blue and yellow turban, its fringed ends cascading down her back. I wonder if her hair is light or dark and I wish that she would unwrap the cloth for me to see. Her face is gentle, the large pearl earring shining so softly that I almost forget my fear. I want to reach up and touch the pearl, but know I will only touch the smooth, cool glass that protects her.

The dark frame of the doorway seems to close in on me as I turn to stare at the space beneath my narrow bed in the far corner. I take a deep breath, close my eyes tightly for a moment, and then run, leaping, sinking onto the complaining springs, rolling the bedding over my head. Slowly my breath calms. Quieter than a mouse, I peel back the sheet. The house is silent, apart from my younger brother's soft breath in the other bed, and in the dim light from the hall I can just make out the pale-blue stripes of his flannel pyjamas. Raindrops trace their way down the window, illuminated by the street lamp beyond the front garden. My eyes grow heavier, and sleep wraps me softly in its arms.

Not every bedtime ends so well. Some nights I slide beneath the covers and weave my fingers through the wire-wove of the mattress base, the metal sharp against my skin. I have a choice — to hang on or to push my fingers into my ears. The sound of my brother's tight breaths tells me that he, too, is listening. Will the ugly noises we hear through the wall come closer, or will they soften and cease?

At the sudden sound of running, I roll quickly across the mattress, my face pressed into the narrow gap where the bed meets the wall, waiting for my mother to leap in beside me and hold me tight. I can sense the dark dad standing in the doorway. In my mind, he roars like a bull, but my mother knows he will not come closer while her children are there to protect her. As her panting subsides, we nestle closer, and after some time we all slip into a wary sleep.

Only once does the dark dad cross the threshold, and in an instant we are out the narrow window, leaving the metal hasp dangling. Mum has always been fleet, and we follow her like baby ducks in a line. Other times we leave by the front door. My older brother sleeps in the sunporch and must slip out the back and up the narrow path beside the house. What does he sense when my mother leaps into my bed? He must lie awake, too, listening for the slightest movement, but who will protect him if he is in the porch on his own?

Somehow or other, we find ourselves outside in the dark, our mother guiding us swiftly down the hill and across the road. Steep driveways lead down to a lower footpath, and we make our way to a low stone wall, a dense hedge rearing up to one side. Huddled together, we wait until dawn, when the dark dad leaves the house. After we hear the truck driving away over the hill, Mum shepherds us home and back into bed. None of us will go to school that day, and Mum will write a note to our teachers saying we have all come down with a stomach bug or something similar.

Once, when Dad has pushed a lighted cigarette into the corner of Mum's eye, we climb over the low fence to our neighbours' house, and they tuck us into bed. We can hear Mum talking softly in their sitting room. Our neighbours are English, and even as a young child I recognise that their comfortable lives are very different from ours. Another time, when we are a bit older, a car comes and we are whisked away to my uncle's house in Remuera, where we lie in other people's beds, exhausted by the evening's events. I sense my uncle doesn't approve, and that somehow it is my mother's fault that things aren't ordered in our household.

One night, as Mum races into our bedroom, my younger brother starts to scream, a high-pitched wailing, on and on, as if the stripes on his pyjamas have risen up to slither through the air like silver-blue snakes. Sometimes at night I can't get the sound of Mike's distress out of my mind, and I am frightened that I, too, might start wailing, unable to stop, until the room fills with snakes and I can no longer breathe . . .

My father, Jack Arnott (left), aged five, with his sister, Jean, and brother Fred. *Jack Arnott archive*

2.

A difficult childhood

My father rarely talked about his early life. What little I knew came from my mother, who was convinced that many of Dad's problems stemmed from his unhappy childhood. We had had little contact with his brothers, although we knew his sister, Jean, better.

To find out more, in 2005 I went to see Dad's younger brother Eric. He had worked all his life on the railways before retiring to Hamilton with his wife, Val, and they swept me into their family as if I had simply been away for a while. It turned out my parents had seen quite a lot of them in later life, and Eric remembered them both with great affection. He confirmed that Dad had had a difficult childhood but, as a much younger brother, he had not witnessed it. He merely sensed an atmosphere on the rare occasions Dad went to visit. Gradually, with the help of Eric and his sister Jean's children, I began to piece together what my father's life had been like.

I did know that Dad's parents, Bill and Frances Arnott, were from Tasmania. Years before, on a visit to Hobart, I had decided to see what I could find out about them. Research can sometimes be prolonged and frustrating, but in Hobart I found everything I needed to know between one set of covers. When I told the archivist at the Hobart library what I was after, he gazed at me, chuckled, and asked whether I was an Arnott or a Dyer, a name that meant nothing to me. He directed me to a book on the Dyer family, to whom, I discovered, the Arnotts were linked through marriage.[1]

It turned out that my grandfather Bill Arnott's father, Henry, had grown up in Arngask, Perthshire, in Scotland, before sailing as an assisted passenger from Glasgow to Tasmania with his younger brother Robert on the *Broomilaw*.[2] On 15 March 1857, after four months at sea, they arrived in Launceston, where they were granted 50-acre blocks adjacent to each other on Carey's Road, West Kentish, where the rolling terrain rises to the impressive crags of Mount Roland.

It took a while to break in the land for farming, so Henry worked as a carpenter, later building a handsome home, 'Glentana', for himself and Dinah Dyer, whom he married in her father's house on 1 January 1868. He was 38 years old; she was 19. Henry and Dinah became early members of the Christian (Plymouth) Brethren in Kentish District. Dinah gave birth to nine children, including William (Bill) and his brother George. As an adult George remained within the faith, but Bill became *persona non grata* when he became a Presbyterian.[3]

My grandmother Frances York's parents were somewhat more colourful. Her mother, Myra, who worked as a teacher, was a lovely woman, but her father Sam was an infamous drunk, adept at smashing up the house. It seems Myra forgave his drinking because he was a severe asthmatic and she believed the beer helped him breathe.[4]

Bill Arnott went to New Zealand in the early 1900s, only to return to Tasmania after working for a while in Whakatāne. In 1913 he moved permanently to Dunedin, where two sets of relatives had already settled. Frances followed Bill to Dunedin in early 1914. They had been sweethearts, but when Frances became pregnant, he knew from the start that the child she was carrying was his brother George's and not his own. It is assumed that he was encouraged to do the decent thing and avoid a family scandal, not least because George was religious, married and had a young family of his own.

Bill and Frances were married on 24 February at the North East Valley (now St David's) Presbyterian Church. My father was born three months later. The following year Frances gave birth to a second boy, Neville, who lived only a year; Jean followed in 1916; and Fred in 1919. There was a 10-year hiatus before Eric arrived.

Dad had always spoken fondly of Dunedin, and I was to make my next discovery there, in the Hocken Library. Records showed that for several years the family had lived in a small workman's cottage at 25 Bridgman Street, Kensington, near the road leading out to Portobello on the peninsula. At the time, Bill worked for the Dunedin Power Corporation as a linesman. One of the few stories Dad told us was about being sent to work with his father, possibly when one of the other children was born. They were riding in the cab of an old lorry in which one of the floorboards was missing. Dad could see the road whizzing by beneath him. He was terrified, fearing Bill would push him through the hole.

In March 1920 Bill enrolled my father at Musselburgh Primary School, not far from the beach at St Kilda, giving Dad's birth date as 26 May, one day out. The original school is no longer standing, but photographs show that it was a handsome affair, with white stone quoins defining the corner of each wall and window. The photograph at the start of this chapter was probably taken around the time Jack started school. He is wearing his best clothes: a dark shirt and shorts, woollen socks pulled up to his knees and a rather natty horizontally striped tie. His luxuriant dark curls, which remained the envy of both his brothers, stand in contrast to Jean and Fred's fair hair.[5] He certainly looks like a cuckoo in the nest.

At some point Dad ran away from home and made his way into the Octagon, where he was found sitting under the statue of Robbie Burns. Who he had hoped to find we do not know, but it seems certain that he had run away after a beating, and no doubt he received another when he was delivered back home by the local policeman. His sister, Jean, told me that Bill never lost any opportunity to beat my father's bastardy into him; he would sit on his chest and strike him across the face, yelling that he was no child of his.

If Dad enjoyed Musselburgh School, it wasn't for long — school records show that he was withdrawn on 23 May 1923, when the family moved south to Milton, on the Tokomairiro Plains.

The town was established very early in New Zealand's colonial history, being incorporated in the 1850s to serve farmers and gold miners in Central Otago. A number of its streets carry poets' names, and so romantics believe it was named after John Milton, but it may simply be a more prosaic derivative of Mill Town. It has a somewhat sleepy aspect these days, but in the 1920s and 1930s it was a hive of trade and industry, with five working mills, including McGill's Flour Mill and the Bruce Woollen Mill, the latter boasting a famous garden. Today the flour mill is a mournful ghost of a building sitting in a field, its windows empty of light, and it takes a leap of imagination to picture it bustling with life.

The town also serviced a coal mine; numerous firms were linked to timber milling, and its pottery factory was graced with magnificent conical kilns. The factory was shut down in 1917 and the kilns demolished, but local pottery could be found in almost every home in Milton.[6] The town's left-wing newspaper, *The Bruce Herald*, ran from 1864 to 1971; it folded the year Dad arrived in Milton, but Bill Arnott certainly would not have condoned its presence in the house had it survived. The town also had the only high school in the area. At the southern end of the main street stands the Tokomairiro Presbyterian Church, designed by the architect R. A. Lawson, who also designed Dunedin's major landmark, First Church.[7] Built of dark grey basalt from Port Chalmers and set off by decorative features in white Ōamaru limestone, a splendid tower rises high above its impressive façade. A relief of a pine tree set into a niche above the door may represent the Tree of Life but is also reminiscent of the fir trees of Scotland.

After contacting a local family through the Milton Community Facebook page, I paid a visit to the town in 2022, partly to locate where Dad had lived but also in the hope of finding any relevant material in the Milton Museum. Sue and Kevin Gorton, who own the last surviving timber mill in Milton, had arranged to meet me and my friend Scott at a local café, but it was bitterly cold and pelting so hard with rain that they whisked us off to the warm environs of the local pub where we could talk at leisure. Over the kind of hearty lunch that Southerners depend on, I was thrilled to discover that Kevin's mother had been a close childhood friend of Dad's sister, Jean.

Kevin directed me to two cottages at 18 Eden Street, one of which was Dad's home during the second part of his childhood. It is hard to reconstruct what they would have looked like in the 1920s, but today both are bleak and somewhat dilapidated, the cottage on the left opening out at the back onto a large, bare yard, its front door directly onto the street. The cottage on the right has a painted picket fence and its back garden (according to Google Earth) is full of trees. Either would have been somewhat crowded with three children and two adults.

The cottages are close to the old railway station, now neglected, but in the 1920s the air would have been filled with the sound of shunting engines, jubilant train whistles and the smell of coal smoke. As the starting point of the Roxburgh line, the long platform also housed numerous buildings, including a refreshment room and a bookstall.

The gardens of 18 Eden Street were of immediate interest to me. My mother told me once that when they were quite small the Arnott children had scrumped windfall apples from the neighbour's garden and that when the neighbour complained, Dad had got the blame. Bill grabbed a jar of liquid honey and poured it over Dad's head, then pushed him into a cupboard and locked the door. He was left in there all night, his mother releasing him only when Bill left for work the following day. Jack had soiled himself, adding to his humiliation, but Frances would have kept that to herself. As Jean recounted quietly at her hundredth birthday party, their father never needed any excuse to 'lick into Jack', and from an early age she learned to get between them when trouble was brewing.

Nor did Bill let Frances forget that he had taken on 'damaged goods'. Such behaviour can have a subliminal effect on young children, and when Dad was in his cups he would accuse my mother of similar behaviour. Bill, however, was a teetotaller, so alcohol could not be blamed for his vindictiveness. Perhaps Bill's animosity towards my father is best demonstrated by the Arnott family book that records births, deaths and marriages from the mid-nineteenth century onwards. All four children — Jack, Jean, Fred and Eric — were originally listed, but at some point Bill scratched out Dad's name.

It was an unhappy house, but if the neighbours were aware of the disharmony, they obeyed the unwritten rule that you didn't interfere with what went on behind closed doors. Dad always spoke with warmth of a woman from his early years nicknamed Queenie. She turned out to be Frances's close friend, Adelaide Milligan. During our lunch with the Gortons, a message arrived asking me to return to the Milton Museum, where another local had left some photocopied documents for me. These recorded a court case in which Queenie and her sons had sued her husband for maintenance, indicating that she had experienced serious violence in her own marriage and would have been more than ready to lend a sympathetic ear to Frances's woes.[8]

But Bill was not without some redeeming features. He was an excellent gardener, winning prizes for his leeks and onions, and according to articles I found in *Papers Past* he did well at cricket and bowls. The most exciting thing I learned from the Gortons, however, was that the Arnotts had had a crib at Taieri Mouth, where the Taieri River empties into the Pacific Ocean, some 35 kilometres south of Dunedin. The little crib was tucked into the bank on the other side of the bridge on the northern stretch of Taieri Mouth Road, which tracks the coast back to Dunedin.

So now I knew where Dad had spent his summer holidays. Scott and I drove out there through a creeping winter fog, so thick that we had no sense of the surrounding landscape until we were near the sea. The Otago coast is often stormy in winter, and even on a summer's day the water temperature demands a certain stoicism, but the beach, once past the more sheltered inlet, offers sand that stretches north; rocky outcrops provide a modicum of shelter, and children can roam out of sight of the adult world. To the south, the white sand stretches all the way to Taieri cemetery. My father never lost his love of this wild coast, and had he had his way, we would have grown up there, too.

Jack Arnott (right), with an unnamed man in Milton in the 1930s.
Jack Arnott archive

By the time Eric was born in 1929, my father had left home. Parents could take their children out of school from the age of 13, and Jack, having failed his Proficiency examination, became a labourer in Central Otago. A faded Kodachrome photograph taken when my parents travelled south many years later bears a tiny cross in ink, marking the spot where he earned a shilling and sixpence an hour shovelling shingle near the base of Kawarau (The Remarkables) on the far side of Lake Wakatipu. Road building was bone-jarring work, not least for a 13-year-old, and involved gathering up river stones and gravel that were then broken up with sledgehammers and spread on the roads.[9]

If you were young and fit, working out of doors was bearable, even exhilarating, in summer, but if it rained you got a drenching and the mud reached knee height. Clydesdale draught horses were put to work at such times, as they dealt with the conditions better than humans or motor vehicles. Later, Jack also worked on the roads on the West Coast. He once told us how he got into trouble when he drove the horse-drawn water cart that served as a fire engine too fast round a corner. The cart rolled, much to the consternation of both the draught horse and its owners, but we could tell that the incident had filled Dad with mischievous glee.

By the early 1930s, Jack had returned to Milton and was boarding with Mrs Milligan, although he must have visited home on occasion because Eric has an early memory of Dad making him wooden toys. In 1933, he found work with the newly formed construction company Fulton Hogan. Jean was now employed at the prosperous Bruce Woollen Mill, and also boarded with the Milligans after the rest of the family moved to Palmerston around 1935, possibly because Bill got another job.[10] By now Jack was a handsome young man in his early twenties, and Jean was proud to be seen on his arm. They went to all the local events together, including the sporting competitions in which he took part.

In those days, local newspapers reported on every event, no matter how inconsequential. The archives of the *Otago Daily Times* and the *Evening Star* hold quite a number of articles that refer to my father's prowess, not just at sprinting, but also at broad jump, pole vault, athletics, diving and cycling.[11] His first love, though, was boxing, for which he must have trained in Milton or Dunedin. In January 1934, weighing in at 10 stone 6 pounds, he won the welter-weight boxing match against an S. Hay, who had the disadvantage of being half a stone lighter.[12] Matches were often held at His Majesty's Theatre in Stuart Street, Dunedin, but the *Evening Star* ran a report of a bout between my father and M. O'Connell of Macraes on 24 December 1935 at the city's Pioneers' Hall:

> [T]he majority of the bouts were fast and willing, although there were only three of the contestants — C. Spencer, of Makarewa, the winner in the feather-weight division, and M. O'Connell (Macraes) and J. Arnott (Milton), the finalist in the middle-weight championship — who could really be classed as outstanding . . . The context between O'Connell and Arnott proved to be the most interesting bout of the evening, and the showing put up by the Milton lad against a fighter of the calibre of O'Connell came as a complete surprise even to those who knew him as a clever boxer. He gave one of the best exhibitions of boxing that has been seen in a local ring for many a day, and his clever defensive work and use of the ring earned him round after round of applause. O'Connell retained his title, but it must have been his aggressive fighting in the final round that gained him the

> decision, as Arnott, with his beautifully moving left, piled up the points in his favour in the first round, and also scored repeatedly in the second . . .[13]

Dad's boxing cups stood on the mantelpiece at home, along with a silver salt and pepper set in the form of little Dutch boys whose heads flipped back to dispense their contents.

For the rest of the decade, as far as we know, Dad remained in Milton, and he was still working for Fulton Hogan when war broke out and he enlisted in Dunedin in 1940. He was 25 when he made the long train journey to the training camp at Papakura in Auckland.

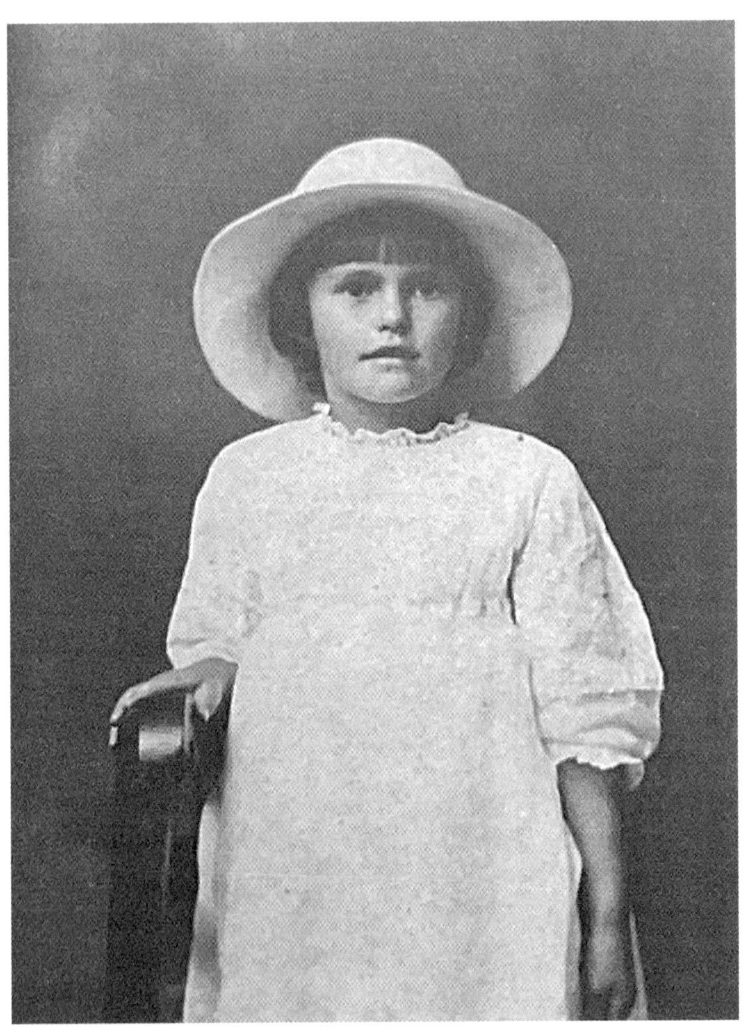

My mother, Margaret Ethelwyn Gray, around 1917.

3.

Life on the hill

Christened Margaret Ethelwyn Gray, but known affectionately in family circles as Ewie, my mother was two years older than my father. In an early photograph, she is dressed sedately in white, her serious, somewhat determined little face peering out from under a wide-brimmed hat. Ethelwyn was the second eldest of five, but you wouldn't know it to look at family photos: in time, all her siblings towered over her.

Most of her childhood in the Auckland suburb of Mount Eden was harum-scarum, roaming Landscape Road and its environs, including the maunga, with her four siblings. At the bottom of the hill, the section of Mount Eden Road leading past Te Tātua-a-Riukiuta Three Kings was unsealed and lined with stone walls from the quarries that were then being excavated to extend the roads of Auckland. Fields dotted with the occasional house stretched from Landscape Road to the Mount Eden village.

My great-grandmother, Louisa Radnedge, had married Samuel Gray in Somerset in January 1880, just three weeks before they departed for New Zealand on the sailing ship *Trevelyan*. Sam had inherited some money after the last of his family died when he was a child, and he was determined to set up a newspaper in the colony.

Louisa was 13 years older than him, but theirs was a true love match, Sam having first proposed to her when he was in his early teens and she was employed as the governess in the house where he was living with relatives in London.[1] Determined by nature, Louisa refused to go below decks when the *Trevelyan* sailed through the Roaring Forties and was happy to be tied to the mast to avoid being washed overboard. Louisa and Sam were setting out on an adventure, and she wasn't about to miss any of it.

After spending three years in Normanby in Taranaki, where Louisa gave birth to three children, including my grandfather, Maurice, they came by sea to Auckland and eventually bought a house at the end of Essex Road in Mount Eden, which they named Ellamore and where they raised seven children. Their three unmarried daughters were later bequeathed the rambling house, their parents feeling that their sons could look after themselves.

In 1909 Maurice married my grandmother, Ethel Steward Watts, who was from Quaker stock, combining gentleness with a determined, practical character. She excelled at architectural drawings and would have trained professionally had she not had to run a home and raise a rabble of children. Fortunately, they could afford a housekeeper, who kept the cleaning and cooking under control while my grandmother turned her attention out of doors. The garden was full of vegetables, fruit, flowers and wandering hens that spent their nights in a chook house designed and constructed by Ethel, alongside an equally handsome hutch for their pet rabbits.

Maurice Gray, who worked as an accountant in the city, was generally described as an amiable man who had a great interest in books and people, although the one thing sure to rouse him to a frenzy was his inability to attach a freshly starched collar to his shirt every morning, and it took the first pipe of the day to placate him. But, as my mother would say, he only got angry with things, never with people. Every Sunday, Maurice and Ethel and their five children walked from Landscape Road to gather with the rest of the family at Ellamore. To get to work in the city during the week Maurice, had only to walk only as far as the Balmoral Road corner, where the tramline into town began.

A photograph, which stood in pride of place on our living-room sideboard when I was growing up, showed him sitting in the breakfast room of Ellamore in the 1940s, engrossed in a book, beloved pipe in hand. The mantelpiece behind him was relatively uncluttered — as it was when I visited as a child — apart from a little lead sculpture of an African boy in a loincloth struggling to control two rearing horses, whereas a small table adjacent groaned with books. The opposite wall was lined with volumes, framed hunting prints, and bound journals that arrived at regular intervals from Britain.

Ethel's mother, Emma, was a tiny, formidable Quaker who came out to New Zealand as an elderly woman. Photographs show her clad in widow's weeds, her pretty face peeking out beneath a modest little bonnet. Emma caused my grandfather much consternation by taking the blankets off the girls' beds and putting them on the boys'. He had come from a home where women were admired and respected, and he wouldn't tolerate it. He solved the problem by building a bungalow for his mother-in-law on the empty section four doors down the hill where they kept their donkey. As a girl, my mother's younger sister Win had the choice of practising her violin in their chook house or going down to number 37, because great-grandma was stone deaf and impervious to noise.

Emma had been on the Quaker roll in Ludlow, Shropshire, and was rapidly absorbed into the movement in New Zealand, even travelling to meetings in the South Island Like so many women on my mother's side of the family, she was a woman of spirit. In the 1920s, groups of cousins would take the train to Swanson, from where the girls would ride horses out to the west coast while the boys walked. Emma, in spite of her years and increasing deafness, happily went along as a chaperone. Grainy photos show them sitting in the sand dunes at Piha, the young women smartly dressed in fashionable cloche hats, cigarettes clasped between manicured fingers; the men in flannels and striped blazers; and a tiny, bonneted woman from another era perched in their midst.

My mother's family were storytellers, and memories of 'home' were kept alive by constant repetition, as they are in many immigrant families. Mum was immensely proud that she came from a clever, literary family: two generations of Grays were listed on the Auckland Grammar School honours board (and were equally skilled as rugby players). Two of the Ellamore aunts had gone to university at the beginning of the century, and the family home in Mount Eden was bustling with bluestockings, engineers, accountants and writers, including the journalist Alan Mulgan. Poetry competitions (which my great-aunt Nell invariably won) were de rigueur at the Sunday literary gatherings. The entire family took part in setting the world to rights. No one was ever turned away.

Given the family's high academic expectations, Ethelwyn's father was disappointed when she came top of the B and bottom of the A class at Epsom Girls' Grammar, unlike her younger sister Win, who was a straight A student who went on to play the violin in a number of amateur orchestras in Auckland. My mother longed to be a concert pianist, but her father discouraged her, believing she was not strong enough physically or emotionally to withstand the strain of performing in public. She developed what was almost certainly anorexia as a teenager and was forced to leave school at 15 when the headmistress tired of her constant fainting.

Her weight gradually dropped to 3.5 stone (22.2 kilograms) and long hair grew on her back while little was left on her head. She was deeply conscious of passers-by who would whisper, 'There goes mad Miss Gray.' Her mother was advised by doctors that Ethelwyn's time was limited, and to take her to concerts, theatre and ballet performances while she still could. Mum fondly recalled how her mother queued overnight for tickets to see Russian ballerina Anna Pavlova perform at His Majesty's Theatre.

Her deteriorating health absorbed so much of her parents' attention that her younger siblings felt they were being somewhat overlooked. One day Ethelwyn collapsed on Symonds Street outside the premises of the herbalist William T. Anderton and was carried inside.[2] Anderton began treating her and ultimately succeeded where several doctors had failed. By the time she was 21, my mother was on the mend. However, her stomach remained delicate; eating continued to be a challenge for much of her life, and anxiety was never far away.

In spite of her father's fears that the exertion would be too much for her, in her twenties Ethelwyn sang in the chorus for *The Duchess of Dantzic* at His Majesty's Theatre in 1934. A sepia photograph, now lost, showed a massive chorus spread across the stage against a painted backdrop, my mother a tiny figure resplendent in court costume and a glittering faux tiara on the far right. She failed to tell me that a fellow chorus singer was the famous Freya Stark.

Jack at the Papakura Military Camp in 1940. *Jack Arnott archive*

4.

A call to war

When we were children, we used to study the photograph of my father standing against a wire fence in his army battle dress after his arrival at the Papakura Military Camp on 16 May 1940, a week before his twenty-sixth birthday. I don't know why Dad joined up, but almost certainly he would have wanted to do something that mattered and that would earn him society's approval. It was also an opportunity for adventure, to see the world and take a few risks. Some thought the war would be over relatively quickly — these eager young soldiers would do their duty by King and country, and soon be home again — although that sentiment wasn't shared by everyone, especially those who had served in the First World War.[1]

This false optimism rapidly disappeared when Germany brought the 'phoney war' to an abrupt halt by rapidly overtaking Denmark, Norway, the Netherlands and Belgium in quick succession. American reporter William Shirer described the apparently endless convoys rolling through the flat Belgian landscape, the seemingly insuperable German tanks and troops backed by Stuka aircraft laying waste to buildings, factories, railways and bridges, before turning their attention to France.[2]

A week before my father arrived at Papakura, Winston Churchill had become the leader of a new coalition government in Britain, and the Italians, under Benito Mussolini, joined the German side. If my father had felt gung-ho when he had joined in January, that optimism was surely dispelled. A couple of weeks later, when the battle to secure France failed, British troops were evacuated from Dunkirk in desperate circumstances.

Those who had enlisted when war first broke out had commenced their training at Hopuhopu, across the other side of the Bombay hills from Auckland. In winter the camp was cold, damp and muddy, making life deeply uncomfortable for soldiers sleeping under canvas. By the time Dad enlisted, however, men in training had been moved up to Papakura, the first New Zealand Army camp to have a sewerage system and refrigerated cookhouses. It also had a hospital and three battalion areas, each containing barracks, a parade ground and administrative offices.[3] The kitchens were well laid out, and each soldiers' hut was equipped with a boot scraper at the door and a mirror by the coat hooks so the soldiers could ensure their appearance was up to scratch.[4] As a young man who took pride in his looks, Dad would have been pleased with this amenity.

When he arrived at camp, Jack's medical record noted that at 5 feet 8.5 inches (174 centimetres) he was of average height, weighed 12 stone (79.2 kilograms) and had false upper teeth. A medical examination revealed damage sustained in previous years — a compound fracture of the cheekbone, fractured right ribs and a broken left thumb, which I hope resulted from his boxing matches. A suppurating lesion down his left hand was currently receiving medical attention.

Jack was issued with his regimental number, 24876, which he had to engrave in his mind, and a Regimental Fee Coupon-Book, 42296, which was not meant to leave his side. He was no longer a poorly paid labourer wielding a pickaxe, but a member of the 7th Anti-Tank Regiment, 33rd Battery, 6th Brigade, New Zealand Artillery. Part of the 7th Anti-Tank Regiment had been formed in England in 1939 because there were no anti-tank guns to train with at home. The three New Zealand batteries would catch up with the 34th Battery only after they all arrived in Egypt. A moderate-sized unit, at its peak only 700 strong, Dad's battery trained under a Major R. E. Sleigh, whose job it was to knock a motley bunch of men of various sizes, ages and occupations into some semblance of a fighting force. My father was fit and strong, used to heavy machinery and could drive trucks — the perfect gunner's CV.

He hadn't been in camp long when he became ill with influenza. The infection was reaching pandemic proportions, and the local hospital was full, so on 7 June he was evacuated to a temporary hospital that had been created in the stewards' and members' rooms of the Ellerslie Racecourse.[5] The *Auckland Star* of 14 June 1940 reported that there were 547 soldiers in the Auckland hospitals, with another 40 cases being admitted that day from the Papakura camp. To try to avoid the disease spreading, the army cancelled all leave and banned weekend visitors and all sporting contact with outside teams.[6] Dad recovered rapidly, however, and was back at Papakura a week later.

His training now became more focused, and in mid-August the first live shoots were carried out at both Tūākau and Whatawhata in the Waikato. Gunners were trained to operate 2-pounder anti-tank guns mounted on a truck deck (en portée). The guns were light and manoeuvrable, but they would prove an easy target on the battlefield as they had no protection either side, had a very limited range (only 550 metres) and were ineffective against the guns of the superior German tanks, which could reach up to 1800 metres. And as it turned out, it proved impossible to dig them in once the troops arrived in the stony Western Desert.

Meanwhile, my mother was doing her bit by joining the Victoria League for Commonwealth Friendship, first formed in 1901, the year Queen Victoria died. In the colonies, the League's purpose was to ensure a continuing loyalty to the mother country, thereby holding at bay any desire for independence and helping bind Commonwealth communities to one another.

One of the League's roles was to put on dances for the young men who were about to go overseas, and it was the duty of its young female members to provide pleasant company and be willing dance partners. Ethelwyn met Jack at one such dance and took him home to 27 Landscape Road to meet her parents. Her father later commented that he liked 'the man with the scar'. However, there is no evidence that Jack, though handsome and full of charm, had become the man of Ethelwyn's dreams.

On 26 August 1940, at the end of their training, my father and his fellow soldiers marched through Auckland. My mother was among the huge crowd that lined the streets to watch them. After parading before George Vere Arundell Monckton-Arundell, 8th Viscount Galway, fifth governor-general of New Zealand, the troops boarded the train to Wellington to join the rest of the Third Echelon in sailing for Egypt.

Among the well-wishers who had gathered on the wharf in Wellington to see SS *Mauretania* depart on 27 August was Frances Arnott's brother Jack York, who had travelled up from Dunedin. But Jack York wasn't just there to say goodbye and good luck to his nephew. At some point he had fallen out with Bill and Frances, who refused to have him in the house, and now he saw his chance to get back at his sister and poison Jack's relationship with his mother. Somehow, he located my father and told him that since he was going to war, he deserved to know who his real father was.

If infidelity was a cause of social ignominy, conceiving a child with another woman's husband was nothing short of scandalous. The shocking news that his father was George Arnott can only have added to my father's underlying sense of unworthiness.[7]

With this revelation ringing in his ears, my father joined the queue of men boarding the ship. Nicknamed the 'Grand Old Lady of the Atlantic', the *Mauretania* had belonged to the Cunard Line before being roped into war service. The troop decks were crowded, the atmosphere described as a 'soup . . . which smelt always of soft soap, warm oil, stale tobacco, greasy dixies and unwashed socks'.[8] A number of men decided to sleep on deck. Even so, many would have been surprised by the relative luxury in which they travelled, even if the best berths were saved for the officers. Once out at sea, they lined up to receive a triple shot for typhoid and two other types of paratyphoid, meaning that for a number of days exercise was limited until the effects wore off. Then, after a brief stop at Fremantle in Western Australia, the ship sailed on towards India.

Now their days were filled with training and drills, including how to use a lifeboat when abandoning ship, calisthenics and classes such as map reading. Equally importantly, they were given lectures on the dangers of prostitution and venereal disease waiting to entrap the unwary in Cairo, illustrated with graphic images that made many queasy or inclined to join the priesthood. There were further warnings not to eat sweets, ices and raw fruit if they wanted to avoid food poisoning.

But there was entertainment, too, and my father would have

joined in with organised boxing matches and other sports. At night, when the light played on the water, many men must have quietly stood on deck and reflected on what might lie ahead.

This relatively pleasant shipboard interlude came to an abrupt halt, however, when the *Mauretania* docked in Bombay and the men transferred to HMT *Ormonde*, a filthy ship from which British troops had just disembarked. It was in a disgusting state below decks, the lavatories were blocked, there was no washing water, and the troops were issued with hammocks for sleeping.

While making their way down the gangplank to see the sights of Bombay, the men caught sight of local stevedores walking barefoot over dust-coated carcasses destined for the ship's galleys. A riot broke out and a number of soldiers stormed the bridge, an action tantamount to mutiny. My father missed this because he had set his sights on the fleshpots of Bombay and had left the scene. The ship was placed under arrest, and a gunboat was deployed to circle around it. The British navy was keen to bring the rebels to book, but Lieutenant-Colonel Wilder of the 25th Battalion, who had also been transferred to the *Ormonde*, declined the offer.[9]

It took a series of negotiations before the troops agreed that they would clean the boat themselves before they set sail. British commanders were unused to other ranks disrupting what they considered the essential orderliness of troop movements, and the events on the *Ormonde* were the first indication that the Anzacs would be less compliant than their British counterparts.[10] No one was charged, and ultimately fresh food was brought on board for the journey. However, when the ship stopped at the British-occupied port of Aden in Yemen for supplies, no one was granted leave.

5.

Egypt

The convoy including the *Ormonde* berthed at Port Tewfik at the upper end of the Gulf of Suez, by the southern entrance of the Suez Canal, on 29 September 1940. Most of the men were relieved to disembark, and they crowded onto the station platform to catch trains that trundled north to Ismailia before curving west to Cairo. They paused at Bab-el-Louk, the bustling main train station, and then passed through Maadi, south of Cairo. They were headed for Maadi Camp, where the Second New Zealand Expeditionary Force (2NZEF) was being trained. Excitement mounted as they neared their destination. One of the soldiers observed:

> Maadi was a lovely sight. On the banks of the Nile just south of Cairo, its wide red roads shaded by purple jacaranda and brilliant flame trees, its big airy houses basking amidst lawns and scented gardens — this was elegance, this was style and comfort. This was for the English community. We were headed three miles out into the desert.[1]

The new surroundings took some getting used to. The camp was laid out in orderly rows of tents, with larger huts containing the various services, on a vast plain of sand looking out to sand-coloured escarpments in the distance. Initially, soldiers slept in the open on straw palliasses atop wooden bed frames. Sergeant Roy (Robert Desmond) Coates (2988) of the 18 Armoured Regiment described lying awake the first night and listening to the unfamiliar howl of stray dogs and the clatter of bats flying between fruit trees near the caves in the Mokattam Hills to the east of camp: 'The orderly officer made his rounds; orange faded from the tent tops; silence flowed in from the escarpments. Soon we slept, but after a while the cold crept up through our bed-boards and into our very bones . . .'[2]

Driver Anthony Madden (36271), who had been a grocer in Takapuna, Auckland, described settling in:

> Next morning after breakfast we were paraded and sorted out into groups and given our various duties. Taking over the camp from the previous occupiers. All our kit bags had arrived and were piled in the centre of the parade ground to be collected and stowed in our respective tents. Sorting out who went to which tent was left to individual choice, a leader was chosen for each tent and after much talk everybody was happy with the company they had in their tent.[3]

Many of these groups became like tight-knit families in the months and years ahead — if they were fortunate enough to remain in each other's company.

And so their training began. Unless they were out in the desert, the routines were strict: reveille at 6 a.m., breakfast at 7 a.m., parades from 9 a.m. to 12 p.m. and 1.15 to 4 p.m., then tea at 5.30 p.m., all punctuated by bugle calls: first post 1 p.m., another at 10.15 p.m., and finally tattoo at 11.30 p.m., by which time men were in their tents. Some complained about washing in cold water in the early morning, while others grumbled that the British Army rations weren't up to the standard of home, but gradually they began to resemble an organised fighting force.

My father would have pretty quickly discovered the central paradox of army life and organisation: the higher one rises through the ranks, the less one is required to know and the fewer practical skills one needs. In the infantry, on the other hand, a private needed to be able to use and maintain all the platoon weapons — rifle, machine gun, submachine gun, revolver, bayonet, 2-inch mortar and Very signal pistol — while also keeping body and soul together with a bit of sewing, first aid and cooking.

As a gunner in the Artillery, my father needed all these skills and more. The anti-tankers learned to use a variety of weapons, including those used by the enemy in case they captured them during battle. At first, they simply towed the anti-tank guns, but these had a habit of tipping over on the rocky ground, so it was more efficient to fire them en portée even if they were much harder to control.

As the men adjusted to their new environment, many would have been struck by the beauty of early-morning light picking out the pleated rock face of the hill behind the camp, and the violet shadows dancing across the dun-coloured dunes at dusk. Both effects were captured in watercolours by New Zealand war artists Peter McIntyre (579), formerly of the 34th Anti-Tank Battery until appointed official 2NZEF war artist, and Lance Corporal Austen Deans (8069), who was attached to the 20th (South Island) Battalion (Canto). Both used tones of ochre and lilac, capturing the dark shadows cast by overhanging porches on the wooden buildings in the centre of camp and broken up by sunlight playing on the veranda posts. The white canvas tops of the tents (some marked by camouflage designs to fool any Italian or German reconnaissance flights in the vicinity) were barely discernible against the pale-ochre sand. Peter McIntyre later recalled:

> The Western Desert was the painter's paradise. In the heat of the day there was nothing but hard flatness, but towards evening the whole landscape takes shape as the shadows come and the colour seems to bloom . . . in the desert each subtle change in the not too-widely-varied colour scheme is something to be treasured and nursed. When you add to this the vast panoply of a modern army, with its trucks and tanks and guns, all softened in tone by dust and camouflage, you have a fascinating world to paint.[4]

Those with an eye for detail would have registered the delicate puff of morning clouds overhead, the birds wheeling over the Nile, buffalo pulling ploughs in the cool of the day, and feluccas gliding back and forth, the stillness prefiguring the crescendo that rose as the mass of humanity overtook the delicate tones of the natural world. At night, as warmth faded with the light, the vast expanse of desert glowed in the moonlight; at dawn, the cold nipped round the men's ankles until the sun rose and the heat set in once again.

Some soldiers had arrived with romantic notions of the desert. The reality was somewhat different. The sand often hid rocks that could turn a well-booted ankle if a careless step was taken, and the heat and lack of water sources were punishing. When on exercises, water was provided in large earthenware pots called zoor, and the need to ration it was constantly drummed into the men.[5] They were permitted to take only one sip from their water bottle at a time, and many learned to refrain from doing so until it got dark, not least because the water was brackish and better for washing than drinking. Fortunately, relief from thirst could sometimes be had if locals miraculously appeared with oranges or mandarins for sale.[6]

Emergency rations — a kit also consisting of mess tins or 'dixies', an enamel mug, a knife, a fork and a cleverly designed spoon made of two parts that fitted together — were always carried in case the company cookhouse and runners failed to appear with the evening's food. The high sides of the mess tins prevented liquid from spilling easily but made it difficult to collect up the contents with a knife and fork without making a scratching and scraping sound.[7] A handful of sand proved effective for cleaning. Those in the kitchens were often referred to as bludgers by the men on patrol in the desert, but the troops were extremely grateful when hot food was delivered. At the end of each day, the men turned their hand to digging trenches, or shallow 'slitties', in which to sleep.

Flies were a never-ending irritant, and sand got into everything, even under clothes and into body cavities. Some soldiers asked to be circumcised, a risky operation when the possibility of post-operative infection was high. Feet were rubbed raw from constant marching, the discomfort only aggravated when sand made its way into boots. Once the conflict began in North Africa, each side at different times was forced by sandstorms to stop fighting, not only because of lack of visibility but also because sand got into weapons and rendered compasses useless. Soldiers complained of sand finding its way even into bundles that were tightly packed, under every layer of clothing and becoming an ingredient in everything they ate or drank. The

My father annotated this photo, 'A snake we caught at Maadi'.
Jack Arnott archive

winds that cause these storms across the African continent have romantic names — khamaseen (Egypt); haboob, aajej, ghibli (Libya); harmattan, simoom — that flow melodiously off the tongue but belie their reality.

When I visited Egypt in April 1981, it didn't cross my mind to try to find any remnants of army occupation from the Second World War. However, my own experiences there immediately brought soldiers' descriptions of Cairo to life — I, too, was transfixed by the crowds of people; lured by the sultry evening air, the pulsing vitality of the city. Cars shared the streets with more timeless forms of transport — carts laden with shrubbery like vast haystacks on wheels, drawn by plodding mules and donkeys returning late from the fields. Many things seemed unchanged since the 1940s. Feluccas plied back and forth on the Nile, avoiding the carcass of a hippopotamus eddying slowly downstream. On the river's far bank, small farms were still worked by hand, a verdant strip of green before the receding sands of the desert where the Sphinx, in all her mystery, stood with her back turned on the pyramids. One of these sported a sign: 'No Smoking in the Pyramid'.

We visited the Al-Rifa'i Mosque in Salah al-Din Square, its internal vastness broken only by the soft murmuring of voices, shafts of coloured light dissecting the space before resting on the myriad carpets laid across the floor. It proved a welcome respite from the teeming crowds outside. But the gently dancing motes of dust were no preparation for what we experienced when we emerged: a sandstorm several storeys high had blown in from the desert, entirely filling one end of the street behind us. A large plastic bag was swooping up and up like a great bird choosing a branch on which to alight. Then the storm was upon us, grit stinging our eyes and getting into our clothes, so that we had to cover our heads with any clothing we could spare as we tried to race ahead of it. Later, reading descriptions of the soldiers' difficulties with sandstorms, I remembered only too well what they entailed.

There were other unexpected dangers for the men, too. One of Dad's photographs shows him observing a large snake dangling from a stick. It appears too pale to be a deadly desert cobra and may instead be the rat-hunting diadem snake — aggressive but not venomous. Evidently, Dad and his mates weren't about to take any chances, and it had been swiftly dispatched.

The 2NZEF was led by the British-born New Zealander General Bernard Freyberg, a much-decorated veteran of the First World War, who took a paternal interest in his troops, many of whom developed a deep loyalty to their commander in return. He recognised that the Kiwis had little time for British class structures. Recalling a high-ranking British officer who complained that New Zealand soldiers were very lax when it came to saluting their superiors, Freyberg famously commented, 'Ah, yes, but if you wave to them, they'll wave back.'[8] Peter McIntyre described his fellow New Zealanders as 'more independent, more equal and in some instances tougher than those of their "home country". Most saw themselves as short-term soldiers and they had neither the inclination nor the patience to accept some of the more regimental aspects of the discipline of regular soldiering.'[9]

Maadi camp was run like a small city, the headquarters' official cable address being 'Fernleaf Cairo', a reference to the koru symbol

From above: My father standing naked at the El Maadi baths; on his motorbike at Helwan; revolver practice at Maadi. He wrote on the back of this photograph, 'The left-hander this end is "him!"' *Jack Arnott archive*

of Aotearoa. Freyberg, knowing what the future might hold, was determined that his men should have as many comforts as possible during their training. Unless out on exercises, they could drink alcohol in the camp when the day's tasks were completed, using the two NAAFI (Navy, Army and Air Force Institutes) canteens. Non-drinkers could buy hot and cold soft drinks, but Waitemata beer was also available, although many of the troops preferred the cheaper, locally brewed Stella, made from onions grown in the flat fields bordering the Nile, which also had a higher alcohol content.

Table tennis and cards were popular, and there was a passion for gambling, my father preferring two-up and poker. The soldiers were prepared to bet on almost anything, and many went to bed having lost their week's wages. The NAAFI's piano was in constant use. Singing played an important part in maintaining morale throughout the war, for prisoners and fighting men alike, and men of all ranks were infamous for their vulgar versions of popular songs.

While canteen tables allowed soldiers to write letters home in comfort, rather than having to balance paper on their knees, Maadi's Lowry Hut provided comforts in more spacious rooms, where drinks were limited to tea and cocoa. For those who preferred something quieter, there was the YMCA, where lectures and courses were offered. Freyberg also set up a camp bakery that produced pies, a welcome addition to basic army fodder. As it had aboard ship, sport played a major part in camp life and Maadi had a permanent rugby ground. By the time the third echelon arrived, New Zealand engineers had also built a swimming pool on the outskirts of the town. A photograph of Dad shows him standing naked, having just climbed out of the pool.

The infamous Thomas Shafto's United Cinemas, a ramshackle clapboard building, held two viewings a night, and tickets cost between 3 and 7 piastres, depending on whether you could afford the few rows of cane chairs near the screen or had to make do on the insect-ridden boards laid directly on the sandy ground. The projector constantly broke down, eventually causing a riot among the troops, who wrecked the already precarious structure.[10] Many men also took part in theatrical productions, those taking female roles often being greeted by raucous cries or proposals from the audience that would have made most women blanch.

It would seem that Dad was determined to shine in this milieu, for he was appointed as a dispatch rider and issued with a standard Norton motorbike. When out on exercises, bikes were attached to frames on the fronts of trucks until required, and the same trucks could return the bikes for any necessary repairs, meaning that riders needed to adapt to using any number of bikes rather than being allocated their own. Dispatch riders (sometimes called Don R) were used whenever it was considered dangerous or impossible to send telecommunications, and they needed to learn a smattering of Arabic in the event they had to ask directions. They had to be trustworthy, skilful riders, and somewhat fearless. Along with their precious cargo of documents, they carried a water bottle (usually tucked into the breast pocket); a pouch containing personal items such as a paybook or cigarettes; a first-aid kit attached to the belt; and a heavy service revolver and ammunition for defence purposes.

Many of the troops moved to Helwan, half-an-hour's drive from Maadi, for training. A photograph of my father riding through the camp at Helwan shows him wearing some kind of boilersuit, a helmet and goggles to protect his eyes from the sand. In a second snap, he is taking part in revolver practice in the desert. Their trainer has a whistle to his lips, ready to blow. Dad noted wryly on the back, 'The left-hander this end is "him!"'[11]

Riding in Egypt meant using the right-hand side of the road, rather than the familiar left, and negotiating the chaos of other vehicles as well as meandering camels, gharries, donkey carts laden with produce such as watermelons, and the horse-drawn 'bint carts' with flat trays used for carrying a number of women at a time. Riders dubbed the mêlée on the stretch of road leading out to Abbassia, an engineering centre on Cairo's outskirts, the 'mad mile'.[12] One road that was strictly out of bounds passed through al-Qarafa, the City of the Dead, a sprawling ancient necropolis where impoverished locals lived in hovels among the serried rows of tombs, or within the larger structures that housed the remains of wealthier Cairenes.

Dispatch riders were the usual means of communication not only with Abbassia but also between the main British bases — their headquarters at Kasr-el-Nil in central Cairo, north-east to Ismailia on the Suez Canal or north to Alexandria. They also collected supplies from the British barracks. It must have been in one of the more distant locations that Jack had an accident, lying trapped underneath his bike for hours, with buzzards circling overhead, before he was discovered.

The town of Maadi had been developed after a railway was constructed between Cairo in the north and Helwan further south. Elegant and leafy, with substantial houses and gardens, well-laid-out public parks and a promenade beside the Nile stretching to the north, it became the soldiers' first port of call when on leave. Those who preferred to stay closer to camp could walk in the tree-shaded grounds of Esbekiyeh Palace and watch the white swans glide across the shallow pools, take tea under the pavilion at the Tea Gardens, or observe the proud mahout and his elephant strolling round the local zoo.

There was no bridge across to the west bank, where the silhouettes of the pyramids at Giza stood out against the sky. To visit them soldiers had to travel north from Maadi until they could cross the river by tram, from where it was possible to hire donkeys. The more intrepid rode the camels that wove back and forth, drawn on by their cameliers. Climbing onto the carpet-covered saddle was easy when the camel was sitting, but an unwary soldier could be thrown forward as the camel rose on its back legs before bringing itself fully upright. Gharries were also available, but it was a struggle for horses in the sand unless they were specially trained. Many soldiers made the journey, drawn to the ancient history of the site, or simply wanting to experience what comrades reported once they returned to camp. It was hard work climbing the massive structures, but the tracings of graffiti still evident at the top of the pyramids demonstrate that many took the challenge.

Another popular entertainment was the Cairo Racecourse at Gezira, which had been designed as a smaller version of Longchamps in Paris. Lines of palm trees stood in the centre, one of which carried a sign depicting a painted clock set at 5.30 p.m. and the warning 'Time for a "mosquito" SLEEVES DOWN'.[13] Dad loved the races, so almost certainly he would have spent time there.[14] When the racetrack wasn't in use, troops used the field to practise defending themselves against possible parachute attack by aiming at the sky.[15]

In Maadi and Cairo there was a clear class division between British officers and other ranks, or ORs, the former provided with elegant clubs where they could wine, dine, socialise and be entertained, while ordinary soldiers made do with bars that often offered insalubrious entertainment that encouraged excess, and where brawling was common. Freyberg demonstrated the egalitarian nature of the 2NZEF when he set up the New Zealand Forces Club in early February 1941, the only club in Cairo open to all ranks.

His wife Barbara Freyberg, niece of the famous British gardener Gertrude Jekyll, was determined the club would be a home away from home for the men, and enlisted women from the Women's Auxiliary Army Corps (nicknamed the Tuis) to look after them. It may have been thought that the average soldier would be better behaved in the company of women. The Tuis arrived from New Zealand sweltering in inappropriate khaki wool uniforms and lisle stockings the colour of toheroa soup. Barbara Freyberg ordered more suitable uniforms for the women, and the green lisle stockings vanished from sight. It was exhausting work, standing while hundreds of men queued up at the counters to choose between tea, sandwiches, ice cream and orange juice, which the Tuis would then have to squeeze.

The club had several dining rooms, and for a small price you could book a room for the night, paying 10 piastres for a bed, soap, a towel and possibly the greatest luxury of all, a bath. There were also hot and cold showers, as well as a barber's shop. A padre was on duty for two hours each evening to attend to spiritual needs. At street level there was a proper photographic studio, where formal photographs could be taken and the soldiers' own film could be developed. Photography proved extremely popular among the troops. The local army newspaper, the *NZEF Times*, published images taken by soldiers and there was a camera club for those serious about the activity. Alongside local news and articles about the progress of the war, the *Times* also published whimsical articles and cartoons that took the mickey out of army life.

For a couple of piastres you could have your photograph printed on a postcard to send home. One of my father on leave was possibly taken early on in his time in Egypt, as he is smartly turned out in full uniform and wearing his lemon squeezer hat, standing outside a garden filled with palm trees. He may have had several printed, because there is no inscription on the back. A second photograph shows him sitting in a dusty street outside a more down-at-heel establishment enjoying a drink with a friend, a large advertisement for Stella beer on the wall behind them. Their pith helmets are pushed back on their heads, and their relaxed attitude suggests the bottles on the table aren't their first. Dad's friend is smoking a pipe, and he is smoking a cigarette. Tobacco was to prove his undoing in later life.

If soldiers didn't go into Maadi on leave, they took the train into Cairo, lured by the exotic crowds of Cairenes, the air redolent with an overpowering mixture of sweat, dung, incense, spices and goat and camel wool. In the narrow alleys of the souk, hapless soldiers were enticed to buy objects to send back as gifts to New Zealand. For many, though, the shabby bars in the rougher areas were a drawcard. Some traditional histories present a somewhat sanitised description of the 2NZEF as 'happy warriors' who treated everyone as equals, but racism was commonplace, and plenty of Anzacs were guilty of referring to Egyptians as wogs (wily oriental gentlemen) or simply Gyppos.

Admittedly, if you were fresh from an isolated sheep farm the crowds and local people asking for baksheesh in an incomprehensible language could be daunting. Excessive drinking was the major cause of poor behaviour. If fares were not paid or if they were short changed, gharry drivers would sometimes get their revenge on the next passenger by attempting to take them back to camp through the City of the Dead, where soldiers feared being robbed of their valuables if not their lives.

Many men made their way to the Birka (Wagh el Birket), whose latticed-windowed three- and four-storey buildings contained a different brothel on every floor. Although the army was obsessive about educating the troops on the dangers of sexually transmitted diseases, my father and many others contracted an STI while

Above: Jack (left) and two army mates on leave in Egypt. **Left:** Jack (left) and an unnamed soldier on leave in Cairo. He wrote, 'A little light refreshment, what' on the back of this image. *Jack Arnott archive*

enjoying the temptations on offer. His medical record reveals that he had also visited a brothel when he disembarked in Bombay on 15 September, but it is more likely that he was infected in Cairo, as he saw a medical officer on 4 November, and on 9 November was admitted to the camp hospital, where he remained for nine days.

His record states that he had returned to barracks the same night as he visited a prostitute, and that he claimed he had been infected in spite of using a prophylactic. He also claimed not to have been intoxicated at the time, and was duly issued a Blue Ticket by the medical officer. In the American army, a Blue Ticket normally referred to being discharged for homosexual behaviour. In Dad's case it must have meant discharge from hospital and, judging by his relatively short stay, he may have been treated with penicillin. The army took these infections seriously; the last thing they needed was for men to be disabled by venereal disease. An outpatient venereal case card noted that Dad was the 956th man to present with the infection, and graphically described the effects of the disease on his genitalia.

During my childhood my father was very discreet about his body — I saw him in his swimsuit, but never naked — so my eyebrows shot up at discovering this about his past. Yet it was inevitable that young men, plucked from home and sent possibly to die on a foreign battlefield, were going to live dangerously lest they didn't make it home again. And while the British and Australasian forces focused on teaching the medical consequences of unprotected sex, thereby putting the responsibility on the men, American forces were later shown posters of the inherent dangers lurking in beautiful women, their desirable bodies hiding a lethal trap — a typical masculine trope of the time that had little consideration for the hundreds, and possibly thousands, of women, and children, who were forced into prostitution.

The New Zealand camp — probably of the 25th New Zealand Battalion — at Olympus Pass in 1941. *Alexander Turnbull Library*

6.

To Greece and back again

The 2NZEF was noted for its excellent levels of leadership, training and spirit, and my father's time in Egypt had given him both a sense of belonging and an opportunity to demonstrate his worth. He was in his prime, fighting fit and bursting with energy. The men knew that fear would creep in once fighting began, but it was a fear shared with comrades, accompanied by a sense of being part of something important. This was tested soon enough.

On 28 October 1940, Mussolini had launched an invasion of Greece, but by January 1941, fierce Hellenic resistance had driven the Italians back into Albania in what was to be the first Axis setback of the war. In March, the Italians attempted a further invasion, while Germany planned its own attack. In an effort to save Greece from this further threat, a large part of the New Zealand Division was deployed as part of Lustre Force. The body of Commonwealth troops was referred to as W Force for the length of its stay on the Greek mainland.

Even before W Force had left Alexandria to sail to Greece, there were concerns about the proposed deployment. Two days after

New Zealand troops disembarked, New Zealand Prime Minister Peter Fraser had sent a telegraph to Winston Churchill expressing his concern that there would not be enough men and equipment to stop the German advance. Yet it was also unthinkable that the New Zealand government would contemplate abandoning the Greeks to their fate, especially after the heroic resistance with which they had met earlier Italian invaders. To do so would destroy the moral basis of the Allied cause and invite greater potential damage than any operational failure.

So, in spite of his concerns, Fraser agreed to support Churchill's plan of attack. Churchill replied that he was deeply moved, and that the New Zealand response would 'shine in its history and be admired by future generations of free men in every quarter of the globe'.[1] As so often in war, such heroic words exchanged thousands of miles from battle were to prove of little comfort to those fighting on the front line.

On 2 March, British troops landed in Greece, W Force arriving in Athens five days later to back them up. The Allied transport ships moored out in the harbour at the port of Piraeus, and the troops were ferried ashore in sturdy fishing boats, known as caïques. The Greek language was just as incomprehensible as Arabic, but the rapturous greeting received by the men as they marched through the streets of Athens, where women lined up to shower them with spring flowers, left no doubt that they were welcome.

The New Zealand Division's base camp was established on a promontory south of Piraeus in a pine forest looking over the sea. Given leave on arrival, many of the soldiers took the opportunity to climb the stone-paved path winding through scrubby olive trees to the Acropolis, from where the city of Athens was laid out below them. They were then packed onto trains and railed to the Aliakmon defensive line that stretched north from Mount Olympus.[2] They soon discovered that for the most part they were to be fighting on their own, the majority of Greek troops having been deflected to try to stop the Italian invasion through Albania.

It is easy for me to visualise my father's activities in Greece, not only because he referred to the Greeks with great fondness on the few occasions he spoke about his time there, but also because David, my son and I spent several summers on the island of Paros, in the southern island group of the Kyklades, in the 1970s and early 1980s, and we also travelled widely on the Greek mainland.

In the southern Mediterranean, April is a season of rain, with temperatures warm enough for the freshly tilled wheat fields to shimmer with swathes of red poppies, their brilliance interspersed with clumps of white marguerite daisies. In the war to defend Greece, however, the enemy was coming from the mountainous north, where tiny villages perch above rocky gorges and lone monasteries gaze down from the mountaintops. In summer, the cooler mountain air here is heavy with the smell of pine resin and juniper bushes, but spring comes late and April weather can be vicious.

The temperatures came as a shock to the Allied troops after Egypt, where they had gradually adjusted to the searing heat of the desert. Lieutenant Charles Moihi Te Arawaka Bennett (6121), who later became Commanding Officer of the 28th Māori Battalion in 1943, was dismayed by the snowy conditions atop Mount Olympus, where his battalion was camped awaiting the arrival of the Germans.[3] For many soldiers it was a new experience — this soft white substance soaking their clothing as it melted or freezing on their skin. Deep snow made walking difficult, the men having to lift each foot in turn — exhausting if wearing heavy boots and carrying both kit and weapons.

The Aliakmon line, where many of the troops were stationed, stretched the length of the Aliakmon river in northern Greece. It had been thought that the rocky terrain would be a deterrent to German tanks, but the real problem proved to be the poor supply of weapons. And because the defence line was too long, troops became separated and communication between each group proved hazardous.[4] This was when dispatch riders were called into play. If in Egypt training on their bikes had seemed adventurous and an escape from the monotony of army routine, that changed in the midst of battle. Riders had to be careful about revving their engines, as it drew attention both to themselves and to the location of fighting units. After rain, it was difficult to keep the bikes balanced if they had heavy paniers on either side of the rear wheel; even moving was difficult in mud that deepened the more traffic churned it up.

Dispatch rider Sergeant Alex Henderson (20818), New Zealand Artillery, 5th Field Regiment, recalled taking a 'prepare to move' message to Captain Snadden (20025), 27 Battery, 5th Field Regiment, one evening. Because of gunfire, the captain suggested taking a shortcut back to headquarters, though there was some concern that because their helmets were similar to those worn by the Germans, they might get shot at by their own side. There was also a constant fear that the enemy would overhear them, so Māori words or place names were used as passwords.[5]

It was perilous work, not only for the riders themselves but also for local people not used to constant traffic. One day, racing through a village, my father turned a corner and killed an elderly woman who was standing in the middle of the road. The villagers apparently assured him that he wasn't to blame, but the accident continued to haunt him long after the war was over.[6]

It immediately became apparent that it would be impossible for the Allies to hold the land they were defending. On 10 April, part of my father's 6th Brigade was withdrawn from its station forward of the village of Katerini to a reserve position north of Dolichi, a 10- to 12-hour march. By the following day, almost all of the New Zealand troops had withdrawn to Olympus, trudging through the heavy snow that rapidly covered their tracks, and leaving petrol supplies for anyone following after. A concertina pattern was set up whereby one battery would try to hold the German advance while the rest withdrew. The 34th Battery was the first to assume this stance, in the company of the Divisional Cavalry. Success in knocking out their first German tank on 18 April must have been some solace.[7] Then another battery took their place while the rest, including the 34th, continued withdrawing, and so on.

The fate of Gunner Norman Mackay (25723), another dispatch rider with the 7th Anti-Tank Regiment, demonstrates how dangerous the situation was. The battery had been involved in covering the Division's retreat from the Olympus and Servia passes on 18 April. While withdrawing through Elasson at the foot of Mount Olympus, out on the plain to the left flank of the 6th Brigade, the retreating column came under heavy Stuka dive-bomber attack. Stuka sirens made a screaming noise as they descended, terrifying the troops below. Mackay was among those hit, and he died from loss of blood on the way to the field station.[8]

A letter written at the end of the war by the much-honoured Captain Charles Upham (8077) to console the parents of soldier and former journalist Trevor Bellringer (523) following his death in Greece cast further light on my father's regiment's movements in

Greece. Upham had had close contact with Bellringer at the Servia Pass when he was in the 6th Field Artillery attached to 4th Brigade, describing the enormous difficulties the New Zealanders faced as they were beaten back. Despite valiant fighting, the German advance proved relentless, as the New Zealanders were now without tanks or anti-aircraft guns, let alone aeroplanes, unlike the enemy.

Upham stressed the bravery of people like Bellringer, who stood to the guns to the last so that many New Zealanders and Australians got away.

> [I]t was the Anti-Tank boys with their little 2lb guns and the Divisional Cavalry in their armoured cars who kept always in touch with the advance guard of the Germans and held them up again and again to let the other forces get away on ahead . . . I knew quite a lot of Trevor's mates in the 7th Anti-Tank Regt, and they all thought such a lot of him . . .[9]

The situation continued to deteriorate, and on 21 April a reluctant decision was made that the whole of W Force should evacuate. Every man and vehicle would move south, an enormous task in which the few roads through narrow mountain passes were churned up by snaking lines of vehicles. If any of these broke down, they were disabled to keep them out of enemy hands. Vehicles on a slope were tipped over the edge. Their occupants then had to make their way south on foot unless they could cadge a lift on another vehicle. It was immensely demoralising. The German planes attacked by day, so most of the moving was in the darkness, adding to the stress. Eventually the exhausted troops broke through to the plains south of Mount Olympus, where they rested under trees or in rubble-strewn trenches between the roads.

Former labourer Private Peter Llewellyn (3541) of the 2nd Divisional Ammunition Company described how, as German parachutists were dropping on the Corinth Canal area, one group was stopped by a dispatch rider with orders to go back because of heavy shelling.[10] The retreating soldiers were surprised by the tolerance of the villagers, whose buildings were being bombed, their roads piled with cleared dirt and battle detritus, and who suffered ongoing losses of family and community.

Ships were due to collect everyone from southern ports on the night of 28 April, but after Greece formally surrendered to the Germans on 23 April their departure was brought forward to the following night, adding to what was an extremely tense situation.

That day, Dad's 7th Anti-Tank Regiment was engaged in one last defence against the Germans, and by all accounts they took a pounding. Their 25 remaining 2-pounder guns (they had arrived with 48) were lined up in defensive positions on the high ground around Molos, a little town in central Greece.[11] Here they managed to knock out more than 12 German tanks before being forced south.[12] The entire division then headed for the evacuation beaches. Almost all the weapons, vehicles and other equipment were left behind on the mainland. Two hundred and ninety-one men had died, 599 were wounded, and the 1614 soldiers who hadn't made it to the beaches became the New Zealand Division's first prisoners of war.[13] Many of those killed in action, wounded or who died of wounds were from the 7th Anti-Tank Regiment.

As each of the groups passed through Athens on their way south, crowds once more lined the streets to wish them well, but this time the atmosphere was sombre. On 28 April, much of the 7th Anti-Tank Regiment was evacuated from the beach at Rafina, near Marathon, 26 kilometres southeast of the centre of Athens. Before being ferried by caïques out to HMS *Havock*, waiting offshore, they took their guns apart and dropped the pieces into the water and destroyed their remaining vehicles.

By 18 May 1941 my father was reported safe in Crete. When we were young, he had reminisced about the island, and we had always believed that he had stayed on to fight there, but his military record suggests otherwise. After two days on shore at Suda Bay, and with no weaponry, it was decided that the 7th Anti-Tank Regiment had more than done its share and should return to Egypt along with the 6th Field Regiment.

The journey was not without its perils, as sailing anywhere in the Mediterranean was risky and troop ships were often shelled. Meanwhile, the remainder of W Force stayed to begin the next battle. For those who stayed on, the Battle of Crete proved to be a further debacle: 671 New Zealanders died, 967 were wounded and 2180 became prisoners of war.[14]

The evacuation from Greece and then Crete took a toll on morale. Sergeant Watt McEwan, who was in the Divisional Signals, 2NZEF, used to go into Cairo from Maadi and watch the returning crowds coming off the trains from Alexandria. He reported that the troops looked:

> Terrible. And disillusioned. From what they told me, Greece was shocking, because every time they made a stand or prepared a position, somebody on their flank would either disappear or be withdrawn and they'd just be left hanging in mid-air. And they had absolutely no air support. It was not pleasant, I would say.[15]

Molos, the little town where the 7th Anti-Tank Regiment knocked out 12 German tanks.

Some later recalled their despair as they smashed up their motorbikes and destroyed their weapons; others described piercing the tyres of trucks and draining all their petrol, leaving the engines running while allowing the oil to gradually leak out until they seized. Hardest of all was having to leave their packs and personal possessions behind to fit more men on the ships.

It wasn't until 12 September 1941 that Major-General Freyberg sent a comprehensive report on the fighting to Frederick Jones, New Zealand's minister of defence. It was presented to both houses of the general assembly on 9 October 1941. He was full of praise for the way his troops had performed, noting how the engineers had blown up bridges and roads in their wake to delay the enemy, and also singling out the sterling job done by the support services (signals, medical corps, reserve motor transport corps) so that most of the wounded were able to be evacuated.[16] One of the reasons the men respected Freyberg was that he recognised the importance of the roles played by every section of the 2NZEF.

The country may have fallen, but no one doubted the bravery with which the Greeks had fought in its defence. Winston Churchill is purported to have said, 'Hence we will not say that Greeks fight like heroes, but that heroes fight like Greeks.' American President Franklin D. Roosevelt wrote to the Greek ambassador on 29 October 1942: 'Greece has set the example which every one of us must follow until the despoilers of freedom everywhere have been brought to their just doom.'[17]

In a speech to the Reichstag even Hitler expressed his admiration for the Greek resistance: 'Historical justice obliges me to state that of the enemies who took up positions against us, the Greek soldier particularly fought with the highest courage. He capitulated only when further resistance had become impossible and useless.' He ordered the release and repatriation of all Greek prisoners of war as soon as they had been disarmed, 'because of their gallant bearing', and instructed that they should be given 'an honourable settlement in recognition of their brave struggle, and of their blamelessness for this war: after all the Italians had started it'.[18]

But any noble German regard for the history of Greece quickly vanished once the country was conquered. By the time the Germans were forced to withdraw in early October 1944, they had eradicated almost all the Jewish population, caused widespread starvation and wreaked appalling retaliation on any partisan group that resisted them, slaughtering countless older people, women and infants across the country.[19]

My father knew little or nothing of the classics or Greek mythology and history, but he warmed to Greece in the same way many more educated men did. The welcome the troops had received, even after their failure to hold the mainland against the enemy — here were people who understood and honoured these young men for their sacrifice.

The respect and sense of debt felt by the Greeks for the Australasian forces was brought home to me when my own family arrived on Paros in 1975. We spent the first two summers living and eventually working on a farm there — walking behind a mule-driven plough harvesting potatoes and planting out an entire field of onions — it nearly crippled me, but the family took it in their stride. The farmers repaid us in food, wine and company, and we spent many evenings sitting in their courtyard, improving our Greek and learning the customs of the island.

We would walk the 5 kilometres into the village of Naoussa for our shopping and when Manoulis, the local grocer, discovered that my father had fought in Greece he wouldn't let us pay full price for anything. When my son turned eight, some of the villagers presented him with little gifts to honour his link to the Battle of Greece. Jack retained a deep affection for the country and its people, and when we described our experiences in letters home, he was delighted.

Back in Egypt, the 7th Anti-Tank Regiment returned to Helwan, where they received a week's hard-earned leave before they resumed training. After they were provided with 14 new 2-pounder guns to replace those lost in Greece, followed by another 10, they felt as though they were back in business, even if those in command now recognised that these smaller weapons lacked the firepower to withstand approaching tanks unless the troops had considerable back-up, especially when defending attacks from the air.

Tension grew as they prepared for the next battle ahead. While the 7th Anti-Tank Regiment was based in tents at Mahfouz camp at Helwan until late September while they waited for equipment, they engaged in training exercises at Kabrit near an air force base in the Suez Canal zone, practising with live rounds at an anti-tank range near the Suez Road.[20]

7.

The Battle of Sidi Rezegh

But this is the Desert — Earth's bones to the old sun lying,
A fit place this for the ancient passions' burning;
And men who were children in sweet green lands are dying,
Bone of their bodies to bone of the Earth returning.

From 'Sidi Rezegh' by Private Donald McDonald, 2NZEF[1]

If the New Zealanders felt some misgivings about future skirmishes after the losses in Greece, according to intelligence officer Geoffrey Cox nowhere in any correspondence or regimental diary is there anything other than a determination to get back to work. Cox, who worked closely with Freyberg, described the 2NZEF — known affectionately as the 'Div' — as an extraordinary body that had a profound effect on the thousands of men who were a part of it. He saw it as a kind of university in which Freyberg and his officers built up a form of comradeship not seen in other quarters, and where it was more common to be loyal first and foremost to your section

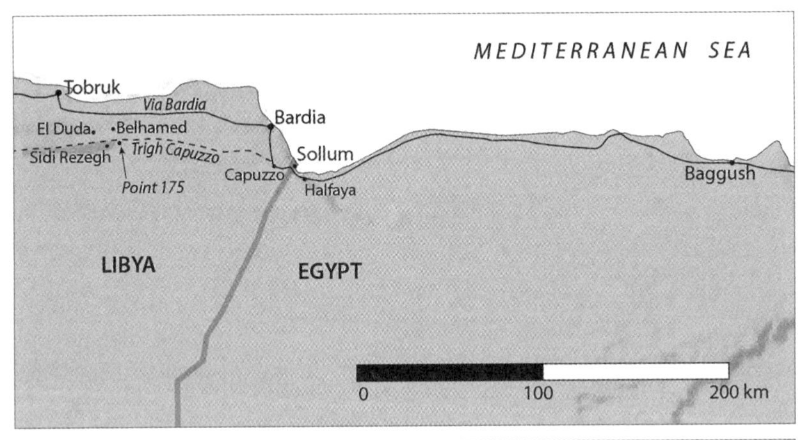

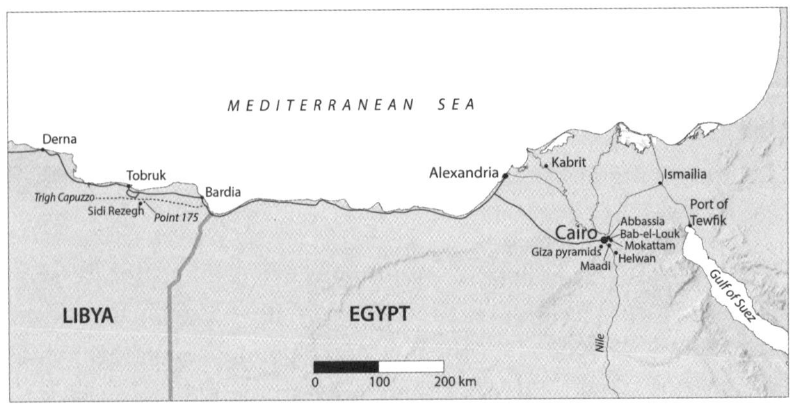

Above: Key points in the Battle of Sidi Rezegh, where the Axis troops under Rommel defeated the Allied Eighth Army. **Below:** Key sites in North Africa during the North African campaign. *Roger Smith*

platoon or regiment. This sense of identity, of the New Zealanders being 'a particular kind of tribe with its own attitudes, skills, its own interdependence, and above all its own pride', Cox thought quite remarkable.[2]

Certainly, if his photographs taken in Egypt are anything to go by, my father had found a place where he belonged. According to records, the 7th Anti-Tanks were a well-officered unit, not grand or dashing, just efficient and dependable. And while their weaponry was complicated — they had discovered there was not always time in battle to winch the anti-tank guns off the trucks and dig them into shallow trenches — understanding quirks of their own weapon had become instinctive, including the knowledge of how to spike it rather than let it fall into enemy hands.

Now the entire force was focused on the next push, which would become known as Operation Crusader. The North African campaign was principally intended to protect the Suez Canal, the Persian oilfields and the passage to India, and the main task of the Allied forces was to drive the Axis forces out of the region. Earlier fighting had left the the Germans' Africa Korps dangerously close to the canal, while an Allied group was marooned, besieged by German commander Erwin Rommel, at the port of Tobruk, behind Axis lines.[3]

Tobruk therefore became central to Operation Crusader, despite some senior planners regarding its relief as a distraction. Crusader was to be an operation characterised by confusion and uncertainty. There seemed to be two principal aims: first, to take some pressure off Tobruk by weakening the siege but not necessarily ending it. This would involve a major tank battle, in which Rommel would be lured into fighting what the Allies believed were their superior armoured forces south and southeast of the port, close to Sidi Rezegh. The second seemed to be to assemble, advance and see what happened.

The renowned British commander-in-chief General Claude Auchinleck appointed Lieutenant-General Alan Cunningham to take charge of the campaign, and in September 1941 the Western Desert Forces were renamed the Eighth Army. Problems started at the top: the Allied generals had been shuffled around and there were radical doctrinal disputes. The battle plan drawn up by Cunningham reflected this tactical debate. One faction believed that only tanks should fight tanks. The Army was divided into two parts: 30th Corps, which was also tank heavy, and 13th Corps, which was primarily infantry and was like a miniature United Nations, New Zealand troops fighting alongside elite Indian brigades, with attached English county regiments, Sudanese scouts, Polish infantry, the New Zealand Railway Construction Company, an orphaned Australian division and South African infantry.

The Axis armies used the more modern and well-practised tactic of combined operations in which tanks, infantry, artillery and aircraft operated in concert. By contrast, too few of the Allied senior officers recalled the first law of infantry operations: winning a land battle involved taking and holding ground. Instead, tanks, guns and foot soldiers were often left to fight separately. Thus isolated in broad expanses of desert, they were easily picked off. From the start, Freyberg inveighed against this wasteful use of troops, blaming old cavalry notions for a refusal to collaborate with the common foot sloggers. He said later:

> I did not take any part in the discussion until the employment of New Zealand Division was discussed . . . then I made it clear that I did not agree with the plan to go out against unbeaten armoured formations unless we had tanks under immediate command . . . I was told I had 22nd Armoured Brigade in support . . . I made it clear this meant nothing to

A 2-pounder gun en portée belonging to L Troop, part of my father's 33rd Battery in the 7th New Zealand Anti-Tank Regiment, Libya, November 1941.

An Allied Army truck drives through wire at the Italian frontier at the opening of the second Libyan campaign in 1941.
Alexander Turnbull Library

> me . . . that unless we had tanks under command we would not move across the frontier until the armoured battle was begun . . . In this I was quite precise. I was not popular, [but] they then agreed.[4]

Similar anxieties were expressed by the South African General George Brink, whose troops were inexperienced in desert fighting. He was assured that they would have the back-up of a whole regiment of anti-tank guns, though this did not eventuate. So, while the army set off in good spirits, they did so with no clear plan of attack.

After grouping at Baggush in western Egypt, where the troops delighted in swimming in the sea when they were not taking part in further intensive training, the New Zealand Division crossed into Libya on 18 November 1941. The border was a rudimentary affair consisting of four tangled barbed-wire fences a short distance apart and stretching for nearly 650 kilometres. For the first time the entire Division, comprising 20,000 men and 2800 vehicles, grouped together in desert formation across a vast area, which Geoffrey Cox described in detail:

> We moved in lines of vehicles seven abreast, each vehicle two hundred yards from its neighbour, forming a vast column which stretched for nearly twenty-five miles. It was a clear, windless day, and the route lay for the most part over firm ground, so that there was little dust . . . It was an impressive spectacle. Early in the afternoon, above the sound of vehicle engines, we heard the sound of

> distant cheering, gradually growing louder. Up the centre of the column was moving a staff car, a Humber in desert camouflage colours. I recognised the General [Freyberg] . . . suddenly the whole column was cheering, with men waving from the backs of their three tonners, out of the cabs of trucks, from the carriers and the gun quads. As the General's car sped forward, the cheering sped with it. It was an emotive moment as, deep in the desert, with no one else to watch, these troops moving forward into battle cheering as if at a football match. It demonstrated not so much the popularity of the General — though that was one element — as the men's confidence in him and in themselves for what lay ahead.[5]

From the air, the convoy moving across the desert must have looked like a vast array of beetles scuttling across the ground. Some narratives stated that the convoy was so long that the first units were in their assembly areas before the last trucks had left base. When travelling at night, the drivers were guided by eerie green storm lanterns, which shone back in the direction of the advancing Division but couldn't be seen ahead by the enemy.

The principal strategy was to provoke Rommel into a tank battle which the Allies felt they could win. They certainly had the numbers, but the Allied tanks were less powerful and were poorly deployed; units were apparently given freedom to engage at will. And they were up against a superior weapon in the Axis arsenal, the 88mm gun, which although old remained a decisive weapon in every theatre for the duration of the war. The guns of the Allies, including of the 7th Anti-Tanks, were no competition, although with skilled siting they could sometimes hold their own in checking Panzer tanks.

Rommel was famously aggressive, impulsive and an original strategist. Like Freyberg, he led from the front and was on equal fighting terms with his men rather than directing events from a safe distance. He also shared the fate of the many men operating long term in the desert who were unwell with jaundice and dysentery for prolonged periods. He was accused of preferring to loot and scavenge than plan, but his reputation was outstanding even among Allied soldiers, who felt he shared their lot and could have been their general. For the first few days of the operation, no major actions took place. Rommel's failure to engage was confusing and unexpected.

Eventually the Axis units reacted. Half Rommel's generals thought the Allied forces were intent on taking Tobruk, while others thought it was a feint. Desultory fighting began, but this was to be an unconventional war of manoeuvre: the enemy could appear from any direction and evaporate just as quickly. To further confuse matters, equipment could be captured and reused by either side, so that frequently action was halted for fear of mistaking the current owner of a truck or tank as one of your own. With air power also limited to avoid friendly fire episodes, it became a fortnight of skirmishes, manoeuvre and, finally, attrition.

A popular notion is that military battle is linear and logical: a matter of attackers and defenders, or, in the desert, tanks versus tanks on yellow dunes. Crusader was none of these. It was chaotic, and fought without fronts or flanks on mostly featureless desert, with very few identifiable landmarks from which to take bearings. Every New Zealand soldier relied on the 3-ton Chevrolet trucks which were used for carrying troops, food supplies and equipment.

The mosque on the plateau at Sidi Rezegh, which had a panoramic view of the desert. *Peter Cox*

These were camouflaged in sand-coloured paint, with a white fern leaf on a black background on front and back mudguards: in this hostile environment, a powerful symbol of home.[6]

The ground itself was unrelenting, rough and stony, as hard as a quarry floor, so that it was impossible to dig proper trenches, and the troops had to make do with deeply uncomfortable, poorly protected 'slitties' in which to sleep. The gunners also had to place their 2-pounder guns in dug or scraped pits. Any attempt at modesty while using the latrines had to be forgotten; many of the troops used what looked like a small, portable wooden thunder box in full view of onlookers, or they retreated to a scraped hole behind a straggly thorn bush.

There was one feature to which both sides were drawn: a long narrow plateau running southeast to northwest, with an escarpment to the north above a road known as the Trigh Capuzzo highway leading to Tobruk. Between the escarpment and the Tobruk defences was a pinch point which Freyberg had modelled in plaster to help planning, a notable advance on the wait and hope, wait and pray tactics of some of the battle planners.

The plateau was only 50 metres above the desert and was devoid of features other than a small, dilapidated mosque on the highest point on the ridge, a blockhouse and a trig point, but it had the advantage of giving a panoramic view of the desert itself. According to Geoffrey Cox, the ridge received its name from an Arab saint whose small white tomb stood on the escarpment edge.[7] The ground had been fought over in the past, and a few rudimentary shell scrapes provided shelter at various times to troops of both armies.

The crucial date in the progress of Operation Crusader was 23 November 1941. The enormously expensive campaign had seemed to be going nowhere, but on this day Cunningham discovered the true situation of his forces on the ground. Misreporting and double counting had exaggerated enemy losses, no one had foreseen the Axis ability to repair damaged tanks and the exposed positions of the Allied forces was discovered. The German habit of abandoning positions in order to refuel and resupply had led the Allies into thinking they were doing well and taking ground. In reality they were walking into a trap. Unsupported tanks had advanced almost unopposed as far as the Sidi Rezegh airfield, but on 23 November they were driven back. The Allies had now lost more than half their tanks. Those that remained were poorly disposed and, it turned out, less powerful than the Axis Panzers.

Cunningham tried to resign and call off the operation. Only the intervention of his two corps commanders, Willoughby Norrie and Alfred Reade Godwin-Austen, stayed his hand. Dramatically, phone wires were cut at Cunningham's headquarters to prevent him ordering a withdrawal. Different tactics were demanded, and the infantry was ordered to step up and do what the tanks could not.

The first objective was the recently abandoned, but now useless, Sidi Rezegh airfield. Freyberg was to lead this push, but he was dealt a poor hand, not least because the Tobruk garrison had decided on an uncoordinated breakout, hoping to establish a corridor with what support it could muster. Meanwhile, the Axis troops, some of whose units had a formidable reputation, were concentrated nearby on terrain with which they were familiar.

The Italian infantry had been tainted by its performance in 1940, when thousands were seen wandering into captivity, hungry, demoralised and abandoned by their officers. The Italians were considered mere figures of fun by many Germans in the Axis alliance;

they were frequently written out of even official battle accounts and their accomplishments misattributed. However, circumstances had changed considerably since that time, and two Italian armoured divisions were used and trusted by Rommel. The best known was the 132 Ariete Armoured Division.

On their way west, the 6th Brigade had dealings with the Ariete. Freyberg had been promised support from the 5th South African Brigade, who were south of the Sidi Rezegh escarpment, slowly heading north — so slowly that on 23 November they were run over by the Ariete, smashed, rendered useless as a fighting unit, and all of their equipment taken. When the expected South Africans arrived, Freyberg discovered they were the Ariete in disguise, wearing purloined black berets and riding in captured Allied trucks and tanks. But the truth was only discovered when the Ariete were deep within the New Zealand position. An identical trick was played on Brigadier Howard Kippenberger's 20th Battalion at Point 175 five days later. He later recalled, 'About 5.30pm damned 132 armoured division Ariete turned up. They passed with five tanks leading, twenty following and a huge column of transport and guns and rolled straight over our infantry . . .'[8]

Another respected Axis unit was the 361 Africa Regiment, a highly unusual infantry formation initially raised in Africa and comprised of Foreign Legion deserters, German socialists, men made homeless after the end of the Spanish Civil War and criminals wishing to prove they could be good Germans. Altogether, they had about the same number of fighting men as the New Zealand Division.[9]

On 22 November, the 5th South African Brigade was visibly isolated in the desert south of Sidi Rezegh. Historians have been somewhat unkind to both Cunningham and the South African forces when recounting the Sidi Rezegh battles. The South Africans had driven the Italians out of Somalia and Abyssinia (Ethiopia), becoming expert mountain fighters in the process. However, by the time they joined the fight in Libya, they had driven half the length of Africa, their equipment was worn out, and they had no desert or mobile warfare experience. Moreover, the Allies, having lost most of their tanks, were unable to provide the South Africans with the back-up they had been promised.

On 23 November, Rommel decided on a dash behind the Allied forces towards the Egyptian frontier, thinking he could intercept the tanks which he assumed would be coming up from Egypt to replace the hundreds lost by the Allies that day. The battlefield was a sea of burning and broken vehicles, a heavy pall of smoke and dust making visibility impossible. The dead of both sides lay scattered and the cries of the injured were haunting. Rommel had planned to raid the enormous supply dumps that he knew to be in the border area, but he had misjudged the situation, for there were no tanks and he failed to find the dumps. He immediately sped back west with his two armoured divisions, joining the battlefield from the wrong end.

All logic in field placings had by now vanished. Rival headquarters were regularly overrun and codes and plans discovered. Elements of my father's 6th Brigade camped one night right on top of the Africa Korps Headquarters, taking 200 prisoners as well as maps and codes, and it was only chance that Rommel and his deputy were elsewhere. A tank officer described crossing four British and German lines: 'the forces were interwoven everywhere . . . I saw British in German vehicles and German in British. The only people you can recognise are the Bedouin and you can't be sure of them.'[10]

It was on this chaotic battlefield that Freyberg set out to aid the Tobruk garrison and maintain momentum westwards. His forces were above and below the escarpment and meeting increasingly stiff opposition. One marker was Point 175, some 9.5 kilometres short of

Sidi Rezegh, a place of no military significance but where Italian forces had decided to stand, possibly using old defensive positions.

The Christchurch *Press* published this account of the scene two days later, well before the fate of the men was known:

> It has been a tremendous 24 hours, in which English and German armoured units fought each other to the death. 'For many miles round the south-east approaches of Tobruk the desert is littered with broken and burning vehicles, overturned trucks, smashed guns, and up-ended smouldering aircraft while all over the battlefield wounded and lost men are sorting themselves out, trying to find their units. There is no front line. English and German tanks met and wiped each other out. That is all. Both sides have taken thousands of prisoners and suffered thousands of casualties. It remains now for the remnants of the opposing armoured forces to reform and wait for reinforcements to reopen this, the bloodiest and swiftest battle the desert has ever seen. I have been travelling over the battlefield, but it is impossible to give news of the fate of the different units. Scattered parties are everywhere, while British air fleets roar endlessly past, bombing and fighting off enemy aircraft . . .'[11]

The journalist had written for a British audience, but his words were wired to New Zealand and reprinted for readers thousands of miles away. He took a traditional approach to the battle, not least in his description of tanks, but the reality was entirely different. Anxious relatives in New Zealand could only wait with dread.

Different records, including battalion diaries, frequently abandon the attempt to construct a coherent narrative of the passage above the escarpment to Sidi Rezegh. All that is known for certain is that as the battle progressed battalions numbering 800 men in the 6th Brigade, to which the 7th Anti-Tanks were attached, were reduced to between 100 to 200 fighting men. The rest were either killed, wounded or captured, and their equipment lost. My father was wounded and captured either on 30 November or the day after,[12] when Freyberg, hands stuffed in his greatcoat pockets, could be seen gazing at a cloud of black smoke rising in the distance: the 6th Brigade gun line being overrun.[13] Later that day, Freyberg received permission to withdraw the battered Division back to Egypt to refit and reform.

British tank commanders were appalled that they had been called to the rear rather than defending the New Zealand battalions. On his return to Cairo, one confided his thoughts to Geoffrey Cox:

> As we came down the escarpment to the New Zealand positions, men leapt up from their slit trenches and fixed their bayonets, ready to join in the attack. They were gaunt and exhausted but full of fight. They crowded round our tanks, patting the armour plating, their faces lighting up at this chance of getting at the enemy. When the orders came crackling over the wireless sets for us to withdraw, we could hardly bear to look at these men. I felt nothing but shame.[14]

Some Italian histories record a win at the Battle of Point 175 on 30 November, just as the New Zealanders record the Battle of Sidi

Rezegh as an accidental victory. In truth, both were skirmishes with terrible losses for no obvious benefit. An undisputed fact is that the number of dead, injured and captured was greater than in any other engagement in the Second World War. Estimates vary, but it is thought that nearly 900 men were killed and 4620 men wounded. Over 2000 men were taken prisoner over the two-week campaign. A week later, the Japanese bombed Pearl Harbor and the whole question of New Zealand's presence in the Middle East began to be relitigated.

Rommel later conceded that the New Zealand Division had played a major part in the near destruction of the Africa Korps. The Allies' main mistake was failing to focus on positions that were defendable, reconnoitred and strategically important. Later, General Bernard Montgomery, who took over the Eighth Army after Crusader, used an extreme version of this tried-and-true method of fighting. It took him a year to prepare for the Battle of El Alamein, and he did not move an inch until the odds were vastly in his favour. Even then the battle took a fortnight to win, but at least Montgomery didn't gamble with the lives of thousands of men.

The Battle of Sidi Rezegh has not traditionally been at the forefront of military discussions in New Zealand, and it is really only the curiosity of relatives whose loved ones were lost or captured in those long two weeks that has brought the conflict back into the public mind. Whether those captured ever heard that Crusader had run its course and been judged a technical win, and whether it gave them any consolation, we do not know.

Whatever the case, as his German captors were so fond of saying, for my father and thousands of others the war was over, and a different kind of struggle was about to begin.

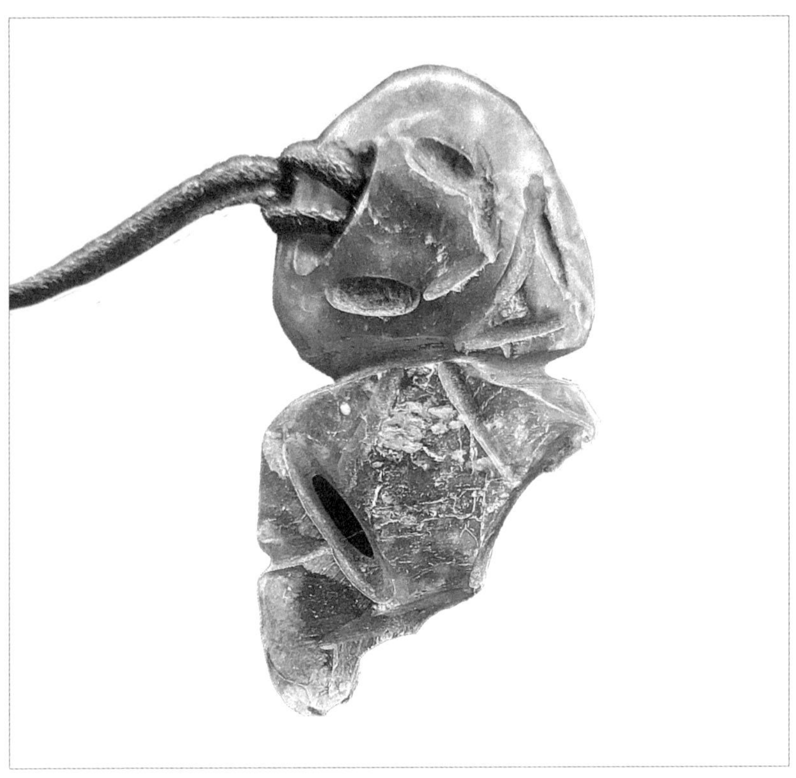

My father's broken hei-tiki, which he kept with him throughout the campaign in Greece, the Battle of Sidi Rezegh and his time in prisoner of war camps.

8.

Capture

We knew as children that our father had been injured when he was captured during the Battle of Sidi Rezegh. He had kept the long shard of shrapnel that had been dug out of his leg, and I used to take it out of his drawer and run my fingers over its jagged spurs. He also had a crudely carved hei-tiki, the bottom of which had been broken off and which may have been damaged at the same time.[1] Somewhere I got the idea that many of the soldiers were given hei-tiki to keep them safe when they sailed for Egypt, but I've found only one photograph of another POW wearing one.

An unnamed infantryman's diary of events at Sidi Rezegh on 30 November gives more details about how many New Zealanders were captured:

> I look again through the loophole on my side and I can scarcely believe my eyes. The sun has set and through the moonlit dusk two hundred yards in front of me scores of men from all directions are walking in among the German

> tanks, their hands raised above their heads . . . A minute or two and tanks are rumbling through and in our lines, men rising from their possies and surrendering . . .[2]

After his unit was forced to surrender, our father told us, they marched a long distance across the desert. The injury to his leg made this particularly difficult, although compared to many his injury was minor. He was terrified the Germans would shoot him if he lagged behind, and he was very grateful to his mates whose support allowed him to keep up.

The North African campaign was considered by the Axis powers to be an Italian one, so the Germans handed the captives over to the Italians, even if on more than one occasion they apologised for having to do so, appearing to have little respect for their so-called allies. Certainly, the Italians were unprepared for the mass of soldiers they had to deal with. Prisoners were taken to a number of transit camps on the northern coast of Libya, sometimes near to where they were captured — Derna and Bardia and, later, Tobruk — but personal accounts reveal that prisoners were also moved from one camp to another, including further west to Benghazi and Tripoli.

Former tractor driver, and gunner in Artillery Reinforcements, Arthur Drower (60719) was captured on 27 November and held at Bardia until 4 April the following year, when the camp was liberated. He described how after the tanks came over, forcing their surrender, they were herded like a mob of sheep to Bardia and put into a small compound with nothing to eat and drink for the next 24 hours and just one blanket between two men. The following day four barrels of water were delivered, and mid-afternoon they were given a loaf of bread the size of a bun and an equally small tin of bully beef. Any objects of use or value that men hadn't managed to hide away were taken from them.

Some men were then marched to another compound, about a quarter acre in size, where, lacking blankets, they scraped indentations in the ground and slept together for warmth during the bitterly cold night. They were joined by their original fellow captives the following day. At midday on 29 November, they were given some hot coffee with milk and sugar (the Italians have always known how to get that right), divided into smaller groups and provided with a watery soup of macaroni, dried potatoes and onions.[3]

Gunner (and later well-known writer and broadcaster) Jim Henderson (24563) was also wounded and captured at Sidi Rezegh. He was deeply unimpressed by the Italians he saw in North Africa, thinking them 'vindictive and lowly, scurrilous people who stamped on your last cigarette in the hospital. But after six months they quietened down a little bit, and we got our parcels and our coffee and our cigarettes, and the atmosphere changed.'[4] My father shared his opinion. Reports demonstrate that the holding camps (referred to as wire cages) in which the men were detained before being shipped to Italy were appalling. There were no washing facilities at all in most places, and the latrines were so disgusting that dysentery became rife, adding to the prisoners' misery. Excrement got everywhere: on hands and all too often on faces when the men tried to brush away the ever-present flies.

Conditions were particularly bad in Benghazi:

> Our quarters were grimly overcrowded, lice and fleas abounded, any food was a disgusting mess, an open cess-pit in the yard bred milliards of flies which swarmed over everything. But even this was a luxury spot compared with the Other Ranks compounds. Here, overcrowding prevented men from lying down; they were exposed to the sun and without latrines. Applications for tools to dig

> latrines were jeered at. A few handfuls of biscuits were thrown over the wire to be scrambled for by ravenous men. The weak got nothing and did not survive, dysentery was raging and nothing was done.[5]

A farmer from Paeroa, Private Wilfred Rapson (67179) of 24 Battalion, ended up in one of the camps on the outskirts of Benghazi. When a young Australian tried to escape, the Italians punished him with the *strappado*, an ancient Italian form of torture, whereby the victim's hands were tied behind his back before he was strung up on a beam. 'This poor lad was hung up until his shoulders came out of their sockets, but he never uttered a sound.'[6]

Although Jack never named the place where he was held, he recalled sleeping on concrete (he blamed this for his later deafness), and there can be no doubt that the months spent incarcerated in North Africa before being shipped to the Italian mainland had a lasting effect on him. Servicemen had been prepared for being wounded, or even killed, but most had not considered the possibility that they would lose their freedom.

Feelings of disbelief were often accompanied by shock, shame and fear. Lieutenant Tom Straker (1537) remembered: 'Being a POW was unbelievable, impossible. You had suddenly become a mere nothing, independence and freedom taken away, about to be carted off to an unknown destination, locked up; to obey dictates of alien people you despised on the other side of the world from family and friends . . .'[7]

That feeling of having become a nonentity was felt by many, not least when they were split up from their comrades. By the end of the war, 8369 members of the 2NZEF, more of whom had been captured in Libya than anywhere else, were behind barbed wire. Only 500 POWs had been taken in the First World War.

Owing to the chaos of Sidi Rezegh, and the manner in which soldiers were spread out across the desert, notifications could take a long time to come through, not least because it was difficult to know exactly where those who had been captured were, or even whether they were still alive. A person couldn't be officially recognised as a POW until reported as such by the detaining power, first to the International Red Cross in Geneva, and then to the government of their own country.[8] The Vatican in Rome set up the Apostolic Delegation Prisoners of War Information Bureau in 1941, to which anxious families could write if they hadn't received notification, but Dad's family may not have known of this, and inevitably such correspondence would have taken time. Unlike other denominations, because of the church's ties to the Vatican, the Catholic Archbishop in Wellington was able to provide formal advice to worried families in his flock.

New Zealand authorities put a lot of thought into how families could assist their relatives after capture. Inevitably, it involved a degree of bureaucracy. There was an official brochure, an instruction sheet for sending next of kin parcels, a map of camps (incomplete), and an acknowledgment card to be included in any parcel sent. Once the parcel arrived, the prisoner was to return the card to the government office to be forwarded on to the family concerned. A contents slip in duplicate was also included, with instructions that both copies be enclosed in the parcel. At a time of great stress, families could at least start planning for how they might support their relatives when and if notification came through, storing approved produce and items while they waited for the requisite official label to be used with their parcels.

Everyone was urged to be patient, which was all very well when you had some idea of what had happened to your loved one. The government stressed it would send out an official telegram to each family immediately once notification of the prisoner's whereabouts came through. This would be followed rapidly by a consignment of the appropriate parcel labels to be used. Unauthorised parcels could end up in limbo if sent before clear confirmation of a prisoner's location came through official channels.

Families also received strict instructions from the Post and Telegraph Department regarding forwarding letters and cards, and clarification that the term 'prisoner of war' referred to those interned in a recognised internment camp, not a concentration camp.[9] The government paid for surface postage, but special rates for the use of airmail had to be prepaid by the family concerned.[10]

Letters had to be addressed using the same protocols the Allies used elsewhere, either to the camp itself, when known, or, until such details could be ascertained, to Red Cross headquarters in Switzerland. Letters to those imprisoned in Italy were to be sent to the Red Cross Agency in Rome, or, if a person was still missing but thought to be a POW, to New Zealand House in London.

There were also stipulations about what you could and couldn't write. Rather than the prisoner's home address, that of next of kin had to be written clearly on the back of any parcel or letter. It was permissible to write on both sides of the one sheet of paper, but no details of the prisoner's unit could be mentioned. All letters were opened and censored (overlong letters put aside until last) to ensure they contained no information — naval, military, political or economic — that might be useful to the enemy. Absorbing these instructions would have taken some time.

In New Zealand, local newspapers published updated lists of fatalities, along with the names of those missing, wounded or captured. 'Expeditionary Force — 26 Otago Names', announced the *Otago Daily Times* on 31 December (listing only local soldiers), while on the same day the *Evening Star*'s list included navy as well as army personnel, making the total 52.

Frances had to wait until 31 December to learn that Jack was officially listed as 'missing', and it wasn't until 10 February that this was changed to 'Missing, believed wounded'. She must surely have lain awake at night imagining him lying injured, possibly dying, somewhere in the desert. Finally, on 24 February, the notification changed to 'Wounded, missing but believed to be a Prisoner of War'.

Dad's brother Eric recalled how he and his mother used to climb over the fence to the neighbours in Palmerston to listen to broadcasts from the Vatican on their short-wave radio. He had never forgotten their huge wave of relief when my father's military number was among those read out in early March. Now that they had tangible evidence that Jack was still alive, they could do something positive to support him.

Campo PG 66, Capua, where my father was sent after his capture at Sidi Rezegh, sat about 28 kilometres north of Naples. *Roger Smith*

9.

The journey to Campo PG 66, Capua

Almost all POWs captured in North Africa were eventually transported to Italy. Many of those who were severely injured were sent to a rough and ready hospital in Bari, but others were sent directly to Naples. Conditions on the ships ranged from poor to abominable as prisoners were packed like sardines below decks. Bertram Martin, an artillery signaller (military number not located) who was captured at Tobruk, described a fairly standard crossing for soldiers:

> We were taken to the ship and battened down in our hundreds, there were no toilet facilities at all, it was absolutely atrocious; three or four days of sheer hell in the boat. It was completely dark, and it was so crowded that if you moved your leg you found someone else's leg. It was the done thing to urinate in your boot, there was nowhere else to go. When we eventually got off the boat in Naples, we only just had strength to walk.[1]

Others went via Sicily, where locals pelted them with rotten food and spat at them as they marched through some of the towns and villages. Most prisoners wouldn't have had any comprehension of the poverty of the south, where the general lack of education and the *mezzadria* system of farming, in which peasants were bound to the landowner and paid a portion of the crops or beasts they had grown, kept them in permanent servitude. Added to that, the ongoing exploitation and oppression by the Mafia in Sicily and the 'Ndragheta in Naples and its environs would have fuelled the resentment felt by some locals toward the prisoners, who represented yet another oppressor.

On top of what he had experienced in Libya, such conditions and attitudes would certainly explain my father's deep antipathy to the Italians. He could never understand why I chose to study Italian when I went to university in the 1980s and must have found it hard to reconcile himself to my growing love for the country and its art history, having not had the luxury to experience it as I did. Yet it was my study of the Italian language that enabled me to discover more about the running of Italian prison camps during the Second World War. A website covers each of the camps, including links to the audiovisual archives of the International Committee of the Red Cross (ICRC), which have proved invaluable.[2]

It wasn't until 2 April 1942 that Dad's family had positive confirmation of his imprisonment at Prigione de Guerra (PG) 66, a transit camp north of Naples.[3] The trundling cattle wagons in which he and the other men were transported would have denied them a view of the monumental eighteenth-century royal palace and formal gardens at Caserta en route to the small but more ancient town of Capua, which had a ruined Roman amphitheatre, among other archaeological sites.

PG 66 had been hurriedly constructed in March the previous year on flat fields to the east of the town, just south of a horseshoe bend in the Volturno River. Always intended to be a transit rather than a permanent camp, it spread out over 12,000 square metres divided into five sections, one for 200 officers, and the rest for non-commissioned officers (NCOs) who had been promoted from within the ranks, and other ranks (ORs). Capua became the main transit camp for POWs captured in Libya, and while the capacity for 200 senior officers did not increase, it eventually housed 6000 NCOs and ORs. Its population was cosmopolitan, as it also included Albanian intellectuals and other so-called 'undesirables' who were sent there in May 1942.

Throughout the war, prisoners tended to be held by nationality, with camps divided into appropriate sectors, but initially this was not the case at Capua, giving rise to extra tension. The NCOs were responsible for creating some kind of order out of chaos, as well as keeping up morale. Inmates came and went fairly quickly once camps further north had been constructed, but the Italians were woefully unprepared for the vast numbers handed over to them in the desert.

At first, the officer in charge of constructing the camp at Capua was a Major Masola, but he remained for only a month and was replaced by Lieutenant-Colonel Guglielmo Nicoletti.[4] Middle-aged, squat, deeply unattractive and a thug, it was clear from his waistline that for him, at least, food shortages didn't apply.

In the months before Dad's arrival in April, a number of soldiers had succumbed to injury or illness. The Italian history of the camp describes the summer of 1942 as the worst period, with men suffering from rheumatic fever, enteritis and other diseases, as well as skin sores. Sergeant-Major Charles Henry Burgess (whose nationality is not stated in the records but who was almost certainly British) was the camp leader when two contingents of 2000 POWs arrived from the Libyan camp of Suani Ben Adem, south of Tripoli, in 1942. Burgess wrote with disgust that the Italian authorities brought them into camp just before midnight because they didn't want witnesses to their deplorable condition.[5]

Above: The enclosure at PG 66, Capua, 1941. The dome of Chiesa di Santa Maria delle Dame Monache can be seen in the distance. *International Committee of the Red Cross Audiovisual Archives*
Below: Chiesa di Santa Maria delle Dame Monache.

The soldiers were crowded into tents, laid out in orderly rows in some sections and haphazardly in others. The larger tents, made of camouflage canvas, generally slept five, although pup tents were also issued, and on arrival each man was given a straw palliasse (a haven for insects) and a moth-eaten blanket.

From the flat, wire-fenced fields, POWs could see low hills rising in the distance (Mount Vesuvius can be seen on a clear day), but the town's buildings were not large and from the camp appeared insubstantial, apart from the two domes visible beyond the wire. The furthest was the Cathedral di Santo Stefano, which has a campanile or bell tower; closer to the camp perimeter was the dome of Chiesa di Santa Maria delle Dame Monache (Church of Santa Maria of the Nuns), which was attached to a tenth-century convent that had been suppressed in the nineteenth century when the buildings were handed over to the military. The prisoners would have been unaware of the church's five naves and exemplary architecture, but at least the dome broke up the uniformity of the horizon.

An immediate problem for most POWs was the inability to communicate with their jailors, so any soldier who understood Italian had a vital role to play. Over time, most prisoners learned a rough smattering of their captors' languages that enabled them to communicate directly, especially when it came to bartering for food and other necessary items such as razors.

Online, I was able to find a wide range of photographs and information about each of the camps my father had been in.[6] The first Red Cross delegation inspection, led by a Monsieur de Salis, took place in the early summer of 1942, when numerous photographs of

Above: The prison yard at Capua. **Below:** The ablution block at Capua.
International Committee of the Red Cross Audiovisual Archives

the camp were taken. They show the grounds divided into sections by barbed wire, corridors running between each, and wooden sentry boxes. In one section, tents are packed closely together, while the scrap of barren ground in the foreground looks like the back corner of a farm where pigs have been left to rootle around. Several bare-chested men are sunbathing in the middle ground, while another prisoner sits alone, gazing disconsolately at the camera. A mood of depression and a sense of isolation are palpable. The ablution block, with its plastered columns and tin roof, looks as if it might have been adapted from an existing farm building, and it was grossly inadequate for the number of men it had to serve.

Prisoners could pass the time reading in the long summer evenings or sit together out of doors, but once the days grew shorter they were forced to spend their evenings in the dark, relying on their cramped conditions to provide some warmth. Red Cross delegates noted during their first inspection that the tents had no lighting or heating, and said this should be rectified before the following winter, as required by Article 10 of the Geneva Convention. The lack of firewood and suitable clothing was also noted. Soap was rare, too, and if a soldier had been part of a work party during the day, it was almost impossible to get clean unless family or the Red Cross included soap in a parcel.

One of the photographs taken by the Red Cross made my heart leap. In front of a tent beside three bare-chested prisoners is a man who appears to be my father. He is wearing long trousers and a surprisingly clean-looking white vest. Jack is grinning, thinking perhaps that the photograph might be sent out to New Zealand by the Red Cross, and he wants his family to know he is well. On the far right is another prisoner who is probably an NCO, although his jacket doesn't show any insignia on the sleeve.

Monsieur de Salis, whose height, dark, wavy hair, thick-framed glasses, light summer suit and dark tie made him stand out from the prison guards, is seen questioning this same man in another photograph. Speaking in English, de Salis seems to be urging the POW to reveal all, much to the suppressed fury of the fascist officers looking on who likely would not have understood what was being said. Between the two figures, the commandant can be seen with his hands on his hips, one forming a fist beside his holster, as if he will shoot the man dead if he gives too much away. They look like the chorus in a comic opera.

In spite of the prisoners' smiles for the camera there was no humour in the situation observed by the delegation. Prisoners took the opportunity to complain that food was scarce, that they were not receiving regular Red Cross parcels or packages from home, and that the camp was riddled with parasites. British airman Philip Green, who didn't arrive at Capua until August 1942, after my father had been moved further north, was shocked at the ongoing lack of organisation.[7] Tents might have been fine in mild weather, but as soon as it rained they became sodden and mud-stained, a poor environment for men weakened by their Libyan experiences. Those who had been injured or had suffered infections had still received no treatment unless they needed urgent surgery of some kind.

The Red Cross delegates were not alone in criticising the state of the camp. The military health directorate of Naples, whose representatives inspected the camp multiple times, felt conditions were deeply inadequate.[8] A document issued by the deputy head of the Italian army's prisoner of war office was scathing about the hygiene conditions not just at Capua but also at several other transit

Above: My father, second from right, and some of his fellow prisoners outside their tent at Capua. **Left:** The Red Cross inspector Monsieur de Salis questioning the NCO in front of the Italian commandant and guards at Capua in early 1942. *International Committee of the Red Cross Audiovisual Archives*

camps, even by comparison with the poor conditions in which many impoverished Italians lived at the time.[9]

The Geneva Convention permitted a captor to put ORs to work, so long as their labours didn't help the Axis powers with the war effort.[10] It was almost inevitable that Jack would end up doing labouring work. At the very least, spending the day building roads was a distraction, and both the Italians and Germans were forced to provide a little extra food for workers. Men in work gangs often developed close friendships that lasted when they were lucky enough to be moved on together. As time progressed, many camps paid working prisoners with camp money — crudely printed notes that could be exchanged for extra rations once a canteen was established.

In their book *The Cage*, former English prisoners Dan Billany and David Dowie describe how Red Cross parcels at PG 66 that were meant to be shared between two were instead shared by five prisoners, which could cause a bond if food was shared fairly but led to conflict if one POW was felt to be taking more than his due.

Animosity was sometimes directed at other groups that seemed to be getting more than their share — although some men later admitted to feeling ashamed by their reaction.[11] Indian prisoners and others from non-European ethnic groups were subject to the worst treatment, not just from the guards but also, at times, from fellow inmates, the guards exploiting any underlying racial tensions by blaming minority groups if any items went missing.

The camp had no running water, so rations were delivered by small tankers from which the prisoners filled jerrycans for their drinking and washing needs. Prisoners were set to work planting, hoeing and harvesting potatoes, but these did little to vary their diet. The daily soup was boiled up in a large marquee that served as a cook house before being distributed to various sections of the camp. Men would carry the heavy pots between them, and God help any who tripped and spilled the contents. At midday the men lined up with their mess tins, if they were lucky enough to have retained them, to get their share of soup and bread, which came as dark loaves the size of a bun. The flour was often full of weevils, but the prisoners ate them anyway, for protein.

Sometimes a green vegetable such as cabbage might be added to the soup, or prisoners sent out as a work party gathered edible weeds from the roadside that contributed a little colour and nutrients to the pot. They may have learned this habit from the local Italians, who even today can be seen gathering wild greens in country lanes. Food, and the lack of it, became an obsession. While at Capua, Dan Billany wrote 'Mrs Unbeeton's cooker column' for the camp newsletter *Clickety-click*. It proved popular, especially because many of the men who worked in the kitchens may never have cooked before.[12]

Only the arrival of Red Cross parcels saved the prisoners from starvation and gave them much-needed variety of flavour.[13] Atta flour, curry powder, dhal (the sheet misspells it 'Deal') and rice were included for Indian POWs, many of whom were vegetarian; they traded tins of meat through the wire with other prisoners in exchange for items they preferred.

After New Zealand parcels arrived via the Red Cross, other nationalities were always happy to trade, not least for the butter, which was delicious, unlike the oleomargarine provided by Britain. Under cover of darkness, there was also a lot of bartering with the guards, who were just as short of cigarettes, chocolate, coffee and soap as the prisoners themselves. The guards were not pushovers, but men could also sometimes escape punishment for minor misdemeanours in exchange for these luxuries.

Prisoners were permitted to receive parcels from their next of kin four times a year. There were strict instructions about what could be sent and how it should be packed, but these rules were not always adhered to, and an item like soap could taint anything perishable. Families desperate to provide for their loved ones were heartbroken when they heard news of the delivery of a spoiled package.[14] Toothbrushes were particularly sought after, as they were impossible to obtain locally, and in brief messages home many men asked families to supply them. Even so, prisoners became accustomed to the morale-sapping discomfort and smell of green teeth and halitosis. Lice and bedbugs thrived in the camps, too — one man described being in a queue for food and being transfixed by the line of lice crawling up the shirt seam of the man in front of him.

Officers were entitled to comforts that were denied the common soldier, such as silk shirts, suspenders, leather gloves, leather canes, uniform replacements and items related to hygiene — luxuries that would have been equally suitable for a holiday on the Riviera. Even so, to reinforce the belief that officers remained a part of the armed services, even in captivity, regulations dictated the colours permitted. A sleeveless vest or polo-neck pullover could be cream, but the only other colour permitted in Italy was khaki; later in Germany other service colours were allowed. Best of all, cigarettes were sent separately, therefore not detracting from the prescribed weight of next-of-kin parcels. Civilian footwear of any kind, however, was forbidden for all ranks, and families were not permitted to send anything that might aid an escape, nor any medicines, including bandages.

Although my father told us about some of his adventures in Egypt, he said almost nothing about his time in the camps, apart from describing the death of a fellow prisoner who was shot when trying to make a dash for freedom. His body was left to hang on the wire as a salutary lesson to others. There were, however, other attempts to escape. Two weeks after Dad arrived in Capua, Corporal Robert (Bob) Albert Smith (3723), New Zealand Army Service Corps, Reserve Mechanical Transport Company, escaped with two others and managed to get 100 kilometres away from Capua, only to be hunted down by local vigilantes and shot, even though all three had their hands above their heads when they were caught. Their killers were later sentenced to 20 and 10 years' imprisonment respectively.[15] Up until July–August 1943, when the Capua camp was closed, five more POWs were executed for attempting to escape, while another private, Black South African Jacob Gedile, was shot for refusing to work.[16]

Commandant Nicoletti was equally infamous for inflicting long punishments for misdemeanours, especially keeping prisoners in isolation (known colloquially as the 'boob'), a box constructed in the centre of the parade ground with a single air vent. There, men were allowed only bread and water. Italian authorities tried to blame the transitory nature of the camp for such brutal and makeshift arrangements, but maintaining discipline was always a priority, and in the absence of regular inspections from outside there was little to encourage a more humanitarian approach.

After the first visit by the Red Cross in the early summer of 1942, regular inspections of the camp were suspended for some months. When delegates were finally allowed back in November, they were appalled to discover that more than 4000 prisoners were now crammed into the enclosure. Many men were still sleeping under canvas, and food rations remained scarce, adding to the increasingly demoralised state of the POWs. Parcels were still failing to arrive, so clothing was in short supply when the nights began to lengthen. One British prisoner referred to the camp as a slum. He described how prisoners would just sit observing Italian soldiers training outside the wire, or gaze over the fields like caged animals.[17]

Dad and a group of his friends were fortunate to be moved north in July 1942, and by Christmas Capua had become an officers-only camp, and the last ORs had been transferred to PG 57, Gruppignano, northwest of Venice. Today, Capua is generally considered to have been one of the worst camps in Italy, and certainly it became the largest transit camp. At the end of the war, the entire staff of PG 66 were listed as war criminals by the British, among them Colonel Nicoletti, who never faced trial.

Once I had received my father's military record, I was determined to visit the four Italian camps where he had been held. My knowledge of the Italian language would be to my advantage, and I was keen to reconcile my own rich experiences in Italy over the years with my father's alternative reality. I finally managed to visit Capua with a friend in 2023, travelling on the same line taken by the prisoners during the war. After disembarking at the same characterless train station as they had, we strolled into the centre of Capua via a modern and incomprehensible tangle of roundabouts. The prisoners would have headed east to where the camp was situated outside the town perimeter. No evidence of PG 66 remains, and when I asked a local, he professed no knowledge of it, saying guardedly, 'It was a long time ago.' I felt it would be unwise to press further.

It was Monday, and the centre of town was sleepy and deserted. The one bar that was open displayed tired panini with distinctly curled edges. When we asked if any restaurants were open, a kindly older woman sipped the last of her coffee before taking me by the hand and leading us round the corner. We were cheered by a delicious meal of seafood, freshly delivered from Naples, which we ate in the company of a small but sophisticated wedding party (the bride was tall and wore a very elegant white trouser suit).

We ascertained that the archives were shut (the waiter phoned on my behalf), but he advised us to visit the Museo Campano, which he promised would compensate for my disappointment. There I was guided around by a charming young volunteer, proud of Capua's ancient history and eager to share her knowledge. The museum's remarkable collection includes displays of half-life-size tufa (scoria) seated mothers known as *madre matuta* holding swaddled babies that serve as the divine protectresses of women and newborn babies. I recalled reading that when prisoners first arrived in Capua in 1941, women had lined the streets leading from the station to the camp, weeping silently as the men marched by, thinking, perhaps, of the dangers faced by their own sons. It was a very different experience to Sicily. The *madre matuta* reflected that ancient maternal instinct to protect one's offspring against the odds — perhaps a universal instinct in the face of war.

Finally, with an hour to spare before returning to Naples, we took a cab to the outlying church of Sant'Angelo in Formis which, following the destruction of the monastery during the Battle of Monte Cassino in 1943, remains the only example of Byzantine religious architecture in the region. Another wedding was in full swing, the female guests shuffling uncomfortably from one foot to the other in their inordinately high heels, their bare shoulders made respectable by shawls of various tones of pastel tulle.

But the real stars of the performance were the men, who were clad in what I assumed was full military regalia until I learned from a gentleman smoking outside that they were all members of the local tax department, whose sole responsibility, it seemed, was to quiet fretful youngsters without impaling them on their swords or blinding them with their vast array of feathers.

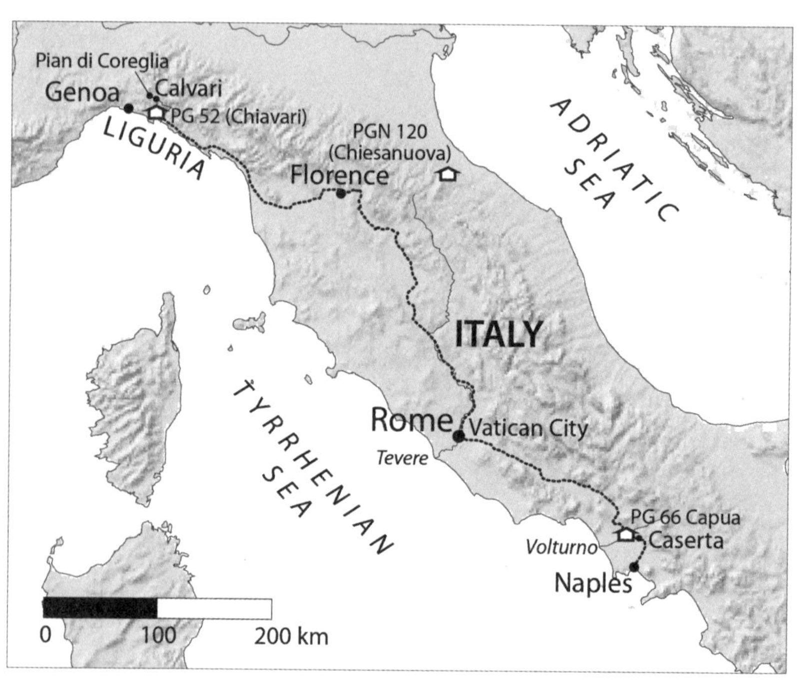

The prisoners' journey north from PG 66, Capua, to PG 52, Chiavari.
Roger Smith

10.

PG 52, Chiavari, Pian di Coreglia

In July 1942, Dad and his cohort were moved north to PG 52 in the province of Liguria, 40 kilometres south of Genoa. PG 52 is sometimes listed at Chiavari in English records, but locally it is referred to as Pian di Coreglia, the name of the narrow stretch of land tucked between the folds of the terraced, tree-clad hills. The fetid train journey from Capua would have taken several days via Rome, Florence and Pisa.

After alighting at the seaside village of Chiavari, the men travelled either by truck or on foot to the camp. Situated 15 kilometres inland, the small town of Calvari is on the Lavagna river, known locally as the Torrente Entella (the Entella Torrent) for the rush of water that builds up once the snow melts on the mountaintops in spring. The camp had been constructed just outside Calvari between April and 16 May 1941 by the 2nd Artieri Company of the Signals Academy at Caperana.[1] Located between the river and the hillside, it could be easily controlled.

PG 52 was accessed by a wooden walkway across the stream, adjacent to which stood the building that served as the camp headquarters. The camp was surrounded by a triple barbed-wire fence, a lighting system and four watchtowers overseen by guards. Both at the entrance gate and outside the wire were armed control units that were also required to guard the weapons depot to the right of the entrance.[2]

The camp had 44 wooden barracks and a large stone building that housed the kitchen, refectory, a library, meeting rooms, a chapel, a theatre and a shop. Unlike some camps, there was also an infirmary, or lazaretto, that had been established in the country house of a local marchesa, which was staffed by Italian doctors and nurses assisted by imprisoned Allied medical staff. The set-up was a marked improvement on Capua. The elderly Italian colonel in charge of the camp was a humanist who took an interest in the wellbeing of the prisoners. Inside the camp itself, the senior Allied warrant officer, assisted by an office staff and other NCOs in subordinate positions, was in command.

The huts looked very lightly constructed for the most part. One prisoner described them as 'jerry-built', an ironic term that lives on in the New Zealand vernacular, while another thought the building materials looked like 'large packing-cases, and some prefabricated, type of Gibraltar board'.[3] As in many of the camps, each hut contained double wooden bunks with straw palliasses, but here the men had the luxury of a pillow and three blankets. In the beginning some were even provided with calico sheets. Water pressure in the camp was low, however, so washing facilities were inadequate and the constant war on body lice continued.

My father was held at PG 52 until March 1943, eight months in total, experiencing the changing of the seasons and observing the effect on camp routine and morale. He arrived in mid-summer, when the surrounding peaks were green, but with the onset of winter they became blanketed in snow. In the long summer evenings, men retired late, but during winter the huts were unheated and the lighting too poor to read by. Talk and song helped to pass the hours.

A more plentiful supply of food had been available at the camp before my father arrived, but in March 1942 there was a 60 per cent cut in provisions because of national food shortages. The prisoners were perpetually hungry, talking and dreaming of meals — not least what they wanted to eat when they were released. Many collected recipes in the distant hope that the ingredients would somehow be procured, and there was a canteen that could supply up to 150 men with onions, dried fruit, some tobacco and rough local wine, as well as fresh fruit in season.

The camp held 3000 men, however, and usually only those who had to work, and therefore received the princely sum of 1 lira a day, could afford to buy anything. Opportunities for bartering were also taken up by men from work parties collecting shingle from the river bed or helping out on local farms. For the most part food was cooked centrally and issued to the huts, and once again hungry men became irascible if they thought another hut was getting more.[4]

There were three parades a day, after which many men went to bed with their stomachs rumbling. My father was fortunate, because in his time in PG 52 Red Cross parcels arrived. He was photographed with two friends after they had collected them. Nothing was wasted from these parcels — the cardboard could be used as kindling, the string woven into ropes (some for creating a boxing ring), and empty tins could be cut up and beaten into useful tools, including blowers — stove contraptions with tubes to draw in air, over which you could cook your own rations.[5]

Arthur Douglas's sketch *Brewing Up*, made at Campo 52, Chiavari.
Alexander Turnbull Library

Fellow gunner Arthur Douglas (60452) took lessons in drawing in his spare time. He had worked in advertising in Wellington before the war, was familiar with design and had a good understanding of perspective, and so he began making cartoon sketches of camp life. An early drawing he made of the barracks at Chiavari is an accurate rendition of their unusual construction. Another sketch — early in that he has yet to get human proportions right — of a brew-up depicts the slope between some of the huts as similar to that in the background. Men squat over their blowers, focused on the serious business of heating water for tea.

One of Dad's photographs shows a similar scene, but the prisoners are out on the parade ground rather than in among the buildings. Such activity seems inconsequential, but being able to act autonomously, in their own time, when otherwise deprived of their rights, was important for the men's morale.

Jack kept a copy of another drawing by Douglas, which was later published in the *New Zealand Free Lance* on 15 August 1945. The drawing shows men on their day off, some sitting alone, others in groups, one getting a haircut, the hairdresser gazing at his client's head, saying, 'Bay rum or French Polish, Chum?' Men gather outside one of the huts, gazing expectantly as newly arrived letters are placed in racks — 'Any for me, Joe?'

Douglas has framed the arrival of the mail humorously, but there was often a palpable tension as prisoners waited to see whether they were among the lucky recipients. Alert to their fellow prisoners' wellbeing, men willingly shared letters with those who had failed to receive news from home. Other men watch a game of two-up, and a large group is shown trading food items: 'Marmalade pud for any

Kiwi's-Eye View

This is how A. G. Douglas, a prisoner-of-war, now returned, to sketch and this picture, giving many details of camp-life, as the best exhibit. See article elsewhere in this issue.

at Chiavari near Genoa. While in the camp he learned
t won 50 lire at the camp's arts and crafts exhibition

Arthur Douglas's sketch of Campo 52, made in 1942, was published in the *New Zealand Free Lance* on 15 August 1945. *Alexander Turnbull Library* other kind but apple', 'Who wants porridge?', 'I'll sell cocoa . . .' In one hut someone remonstrates, 'You've burnt the toast again, you fool', while outside another man returns with his bowl of soup, gazing into it glumly and muttering, 'Multi acqua!' (mostly water).

A cardboard crate is being used as the wickets for a cricket match; on a rooftop a guard is watching a prisoner as he paints — 'I chose the colour myself' — while on another a wooden baton is removed for firewood: 'Must have the ol' brew'. At the rear of the camp men queue at the library — 'Last time I got a book on Dieting' — while inside someone jokes, 'Can I walk you home through the park?' 'Not bloody likely'.

In the foreground, a man carrying folded laundry shoos away a dog that has come in from the village in the hope of a fallen scrap of food, while a soldier asks a patrolling guard if he has finished yet. Phrases of Italian demonstrate the smattering of the language learned by the prisoners; no doubt some of the guards learned some English in return.

This simple cartoon already illustrates a highly sophisticated perspective: Douglas has drawn the scene from a bird's eye view; that is, from a vantage point above the camp — an area Douglas may have visited when prisoners were sometimes permitted to walk in the woods under guard on a Sunday. This technique has been used since the Renaissance, when it is thought that the Flemish painter Giusto Utens used it in his lunette paintings of the 17 Medici palazzi in Florence and Tuscany.[6]

When Douglas's cartoon was reproduced in the *Free Lance* in 1945, the accompanying article gave his address as Dolly Varden (Paremata) Bay, Plimmerton, and it was noted that the original drawing had been claimed by the Italian Carabinieri, and so 'Mr Douglas drew it again, from memory, in Germany two years later'.

Above: Dad, at left, with two fellow prisoners at Chiavari. Judging by their heavy clothing, the photograph was taken in autumn. **Below:** An illicit photograph showing men at Chiavari with their boilers. *Jack Arnott archive*

In 2023, the Aigantighe Art Gallery in Tīmaru published the catalogue of an invaluable archive that had been donated to its collection. It includes paintings and drawings by Tīmaru schoolteacher Sergeant John Edward 'Jock' Fraser (11418), who was also captured at Sidi Rezegh. He made many sketches and watercolours of daily life at Chiavari, capturing the surrounding landscape and three- to four-storeyed village houses. An intimate sketch shows a prisoner sleeping in his narrow bunk covered by a greatcoat, his mess tin resting on the floor and his water bottle hanging from a nail.[7]

One drawing that differs from the others suggests that there may have been art books in the camp library, notably one that reproduced German artist Albrecht Dürer's revolutionary masterpiece *Great Piece of Turf*. Dürer created the work in 1503, having lain face down to closely observe the clump of wild plants directly in front of him, which included cock's-foot, creeping bent, smooth meadowgrass, daisy, dandelion, germander speedwell, greater plantain, hound's-tongue and yarrow.[8]

Fraser has taken the same viewpoint in his ink drawing 'Arrangement with Barbed Wire', 1942, which captures a line of spring poppies that have sprung up among perimeter weeds. It is poignant on many levels, some of the weeds being edible and the poppies suggestive of the fallen on Flanders Fields. But it is the vertical and horizontal strands of barbed wire which indicate that the artist's eye is that of a prisoner.[9] The poppies were growing in front of two cottages belonging to prison guards, directly behind the wire and beneath the terraced hillside, and can also be seen in a curious photograph in my father's collection. The photo must have been taken surreptitiously, perhaps from inside a jacket or a pocket, hence the tilt of the ground.

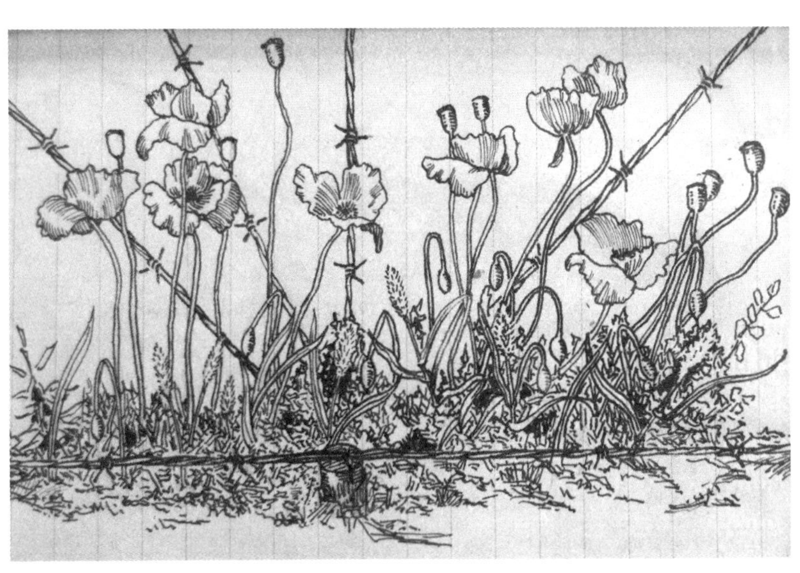

Jock Fraser's drawing *Flower Arrangement with Barbed Wire*, made at Chiavari in 1942. *Aigantighe Art Gallery, Tīmaru, reproduced courtesy of the artist's estate*

Above: The perimeter fence and cottages at Chiavari. **Below:** My father wrote on the back of this photograph, 'All Beds and Gear out for a Search, Campo 52, Chiavari'. *Jack Arnott archive*

Wherever possible prisoners made their own gardens to supplement their diets, ordering seeds from the Red Cross or bartering for them with locals. In October 1942, families in New Zealand learned that POWs would soon be provided with packets of herbs from England thanks to a new initiative by the Red Cross:

> Widows and pensioners with small cottage gardens as well as from the herb gardens of manor houses have all yielded their contributions . . . There is no nourishment in thyme, sage, mint, parsley, and bay leaf, but their value is quite out of proportion to the amount of space they take up, for they help to make savoury dishes, and so will elleviate [sic] the monotony of prison diet.[10]

Reminders of life outside the camp were welcome. Local Italian newspapers, which prisoners banded together to buy, became important sources of information, even if not everything in them could be believed. Eventually, requests were made to the Red Cross for sports equipment, books and even musical instruments. Somehow Chiavari ended up with a piano — a photograph shows a group having a singsong, accompanied by a piano accordion. Music of any kind was extremely popular, and singing, including of the crude adaptations of popular tunes the men had learned in Egypt, lifted their spirits.[11]

Once a prisoner arrived at a permanent camp, he was permitted to write a message that would be broadcast worldwide by the Vatican Radio. Those who had time to consider what their needs were, over and above food, might construct a message in the allotted 12 words that ensured they received what they required. New Zealand Captain Malcolm Mason (30959), who was determined to finish his interrupted education, wrote: 'Unwounded, well. Please send economics study books, meat concentrate and caramels. Love.'[12]

To meet the need for mental stimulation, a range of other activities — mirrored in similar ways in most of the permanent camps — was organised. Lectures on all kinds of subjects were given, often recorded in notebooks acquired from the canteen. Some men turned to religion, while others with a more practical bent learned about farming, among other subjects.

One prisoner who was to move to the next two camps in my father's and Arthur Douglas's company was Lance Sergeant George Lochhead (8282), who had worked as a grocer's assistant in Invercargill before the war. In the camp, Lochhead took up smoking, as it helped to assuage hunger pangs, and he recalled later that sometimes for breakfast he would make do with a cup of mint tea, a cigarette and a look out the window.[13] He also enjoyed the concerts and other performances put on by his fellow prisoners.

Every tin of food in his parcels was put to good use, creating stage props that included hammers, spectacles and wine glasses. He proudly recalled that at Christmas 1942 the prisoners performed *The Messiah*; earlier they had put on *Pygmalion*, *Of Mice and Men* and *Les Misérables*. Along with the remarkable production of props and costumes — women's costumes invariably included very large artificial breasts — rehearsals helped to fill the long evenings as winter began to close in. I don't know if Dad ever performed, but he was blessed with a good singing voice and would certainly have enjoyed the entertainment.[14]

As much as diversions such as these helped with morale, it was the packages from family, friends and community that really improved individual wellbeing, reminding the men that they were still loved and not forgotten. My grandmother Frances wrote to Jack, of course, but according to my cousins the most assiduous writer was his sister, Jean. Not all letters would have reached him. He may have hidden those that did come through, but none of them survived the war and many were probably put to practical use in the latrines.

One photograph from home that did survive into peacetime was taken in Wellington and shows Jean striding along with her landlady and son. It is a bright summer's day, but a classic sou'-wester seems to be blowing and both women are clutching their hats. Arthur Douglas also made sketches from my father's photographs, including one of Frances, which somehow also managed to survive the war, sunlike the original photograph from which it was taken. The sketch is signed and dated 1943, so we can't be sure whether Douglas drew it at PG 52, Chiavari, or in one of the next two camps they were in together.

ORs were usually allowed to write two letters and four postcards a month, a task that required them to focus on trying to project something positive about their situations. This pattern was set back in New Zealand, where the pamphlet *Prisoners of War*, which had been established in January 1942 by the Prisoners of War Enquiry Office of the Joint Council of the Order of St John and the New Zealand Red Cross Society in Wellington, advised people to be circumspect about what they included in letters — to be positive about a film they'd seen or a good book, or to describe what they were planting in the garden. Wives were advised to talk about clothes that had been mended, how a child was progressing and how they were saving carefully for their loved one's return. They were not to write about anything that might make a prisoner feel dejected. Descriptions of wasted food, minor illnesses, arguments and other fallings-out, money ill-spent — or, worse still, lost — and even inadvertent breakages at home were not recommended.[15]

Left: Arthur Douglas's drawing of my grandmother Frances Arnott, made for my father while they were at Chiavari together in 1943. **Right:** Dad's sister, Jean (left), and her landlady trying to keep their hats on in Wellington's wind some time between 1944 and 1945. *Jack Arnott archive*

A sizable pamphlet, the *Prisoners of War News Sheet* mostly reproduced letters sent to families from prisoners. Many more seem to have been published from Germany than from Italy, and a good number were by officers who were exempt from work and so had more time to write. Reading through them, it becomes apparent that most prisoners put a gallant slant on their predicaments. They talked incessantly about Red Cross parcels, and how invaluable they were, though there were also wry accounts of blankets and socks that had been posted only to arrive full of moth holes. Descriptions of sports and other activities also featured large.

One officer complained about the difficulty he had studying as it was so rowdy in the huts, while others outlined their attempts at gardening. It all seemed jolly hockey sticks, as if they were describing their time at boarding school or holiday camp, but the men knew their letters would be censored, and so avoided criticising or giving too much away about prison life. Another favourite strategy was to refer to old acquaintances and friends in the same camp so that information could then be shared with their concerned families.

At PG 52, roll-call every morning was carried out inside the huts, rather than on the parade ground, and so prisoners often didn't bother getting dressed until afterwards. An intriguing photograph among Dad's collection is a print of one taken by Gunner Wilfred (Curly) Albert Weakley (61103), which is held at the National Library.[16] Weakley, who was captured at Sidi Rezegh, had been a storeman and packer in civilian life. He titled the photograph 'All Beds and Gear out for a Search, Campo 52, Chiavari'. It shows one of the searches regularly undertaken for contraband or any kind of map that might indicate a planned escape. The bunks have been removed and taken apart, and it is clear that slats have already been taken out of some beds to be used as firewood for brewing tea.

It is not known where these photographs were originally printed. Certainly, Jack's photograph is a lot grainier than the one held at the Turnbull Library, but it's hard to imagine any printing equipment being allowed in the camps. We do know, however, that Weakley took the photograph with his 35mm Kodak Retina camera, which he had hidden at his time of capture by strapping it to the inside of his leg. Later, he created what looked to be a water bottle out of Canadian dried milk tins and hid the camera in that.[17] Weakley's camera and its case are held today at the Waiouru Army Museum.

In March 1943, Dad and many other inmates packed up once more and moved across northern Italy, bringing what had been a relatively agreeable experience to an end. Later that same year, PG 52 was emptied of all its remaining Allied prisoners, and local Jewish people were held there before being shipped to Auschwitz, where many lost their lives. Today, the huts have gone, and only a stone building remains, its pale plastered walls peeling and barred windows giving a glimpse of rubbish strewn inside.

The two cottages outside the camp are still there, and on the fence there is a memorial to those who died in the Holocaust. No mention is made of the Allies who had also been imprisoned there, although the Red Cross website has a chart that indicates the multi-cultural nature of the camp in 1943.[18]

Campo PG 52 is the only Italian camp site I have never been able to get close to. On the two occasions I travelled through Chiavari, either heading south to Florence or north to Genoa, I was without a car and had to make do with gazing up at the tree-clad hills either side of the valley behind the railway station. Dad's little collection of photographs, along with the prisoners' drawings, must suffice to show what the camp was like.

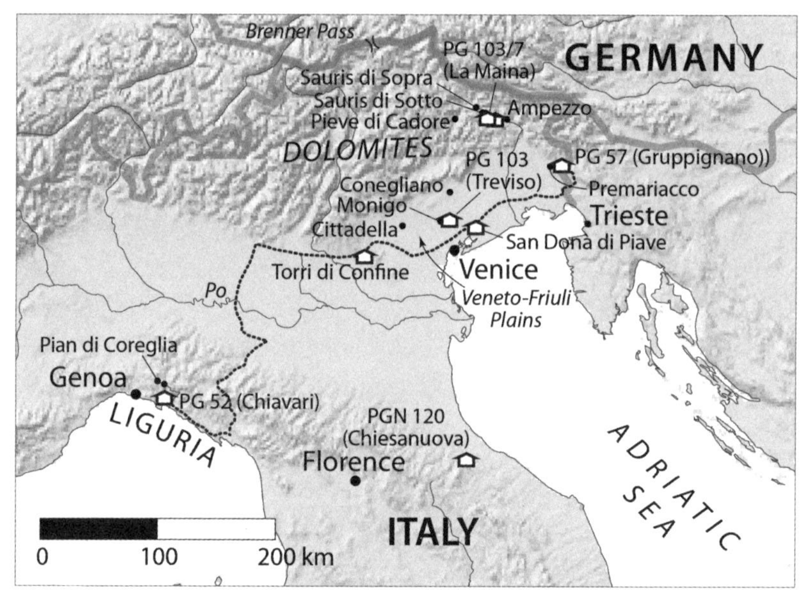

Route of the prisoners' journey in 1943 from Chiavari to PG 57, Gruppignano. *Roger Smith*

11.

PG 57, Gruppignano

On 31 March 1943, the Rome commission informed the Arnott family that Jack was now listed at Campo PG 57, Gruppignano, near Udine in the municipality of Premariacco, about 60 kilometres northwest of Trieste and not far from the Austrian border. Approximately 320 kilometres by rail from Chiavari, today the journey takes only seven and a half hours, but it would have taken considerably longer in 1943. Snow visible on the nearby mountains was only beginning to melt when the men arrived, making their initial routine delousing a chilly affair.

Many POW camps had been utilised as such in the First World War, but Gruppignano was purpose built in May 1941 to deal with the ever-increasing number of captured Allies, particularly Australians and New Zealanders. The Australian POWs captured in Greece and Crete built the latrines. Its inmates included British, Canadian, Cypriot, Nepali (Gorkhali), Greek, Indian, Palestinian and South African prisoners, and one isolated Chinese man, Ah Kai.[1] By June 1942, it held more than 3500 prisoners in four compounds, and preparations were being made to deal with another influx.[2]

Supposedly escape proof, the camp had a 5-metre-high squared barbed-wire fence followed by a double concertina obstacle, and then a high double-apron fence of barbed wire with concertina wire under each apron. The entire camp was lit by powerful arc lights and manned by closely placed machine-gun posts, as well as moving sentries.[3]

Despite some of its inmates being moved out to work camps, PG 57 was overcrowded, and soon a new sector had to be constructed. New Zealand government records painted a sanitised view of the camp in July 1942, describing it as well organised at every level. Some prisoners hotly denied this, arguing that they didn't receive the parcels they should have, and that the canteen mainly stocked toothpaste and razors — although there was once a sack of onions surplus to the Italians' requirements.[4]

There is now little evidence of the layout of the camp, but photographs taken at the time show barracks laid out in serried rows and a dirt road between the different compounds marked by grass beds, with small gardens ornamented with precise rows of white-painted stones placed by the prisoners. Young saplings had been planted along the wire, suggesting that the camp was intended to be there for a good length of time. On the opposite side of the road leading to the camp a deep ditch (which still remains) had been cut to manage springtime flooding.[5]

Gruppignano was run by Vittorio Calcaterra, and the official New Zealand war history of the camp includes personal recollections from former POWs that paint a more detailed picture:

> Every prisoner-of-war camp in Italy had a squad of *Carabinieri Reali*, the police force whose specialist efficiency preceded the advent of Fascism. These men were responsible for security, seemed to be able to over-rule

the Army commandant of camps, no matter what his rank, conducted the most rigorous and unexpected searches of personal belongings, and sometimes treated prisoners with the brutality which presumably had become habitual to them in dealing with civil offenders. At Gruppignano the commandant was himself a colonel in the *Carabinieri Reali*; he was also military governor of Udine and an ardent Fascist. This man, Calcaterra, prided himself on the strictness of his discipline, and the thirty cells at Gruppignano were never empty. Had he not been killed by Italian partisans; he would probably have faced war-crimes charges. Many prisoners had something approaching respect for this would-be ogre, and one recorded his satisfaction that Calcaterra at the fall of Mussolini did not, like so many Fascists, attempt to change his coat.

Atrocities were committed in this camp — a man who had got drunk was shot by a *carabiniere* while being helped back to his hut, and another was shot while getting wood after dark —and in general discipline was childishly pin-pricking. Men whose faces twitched on roll-call parade went straight to the cells, without trial or inquiry. If too much talking went on at night in any hut, the *Carabinieri* took several men at random and put them in the cells. Life in the camp's cells was not as bad as it might have been, as extra food and cigarettes were smuggled in by friends, the cigarettes being hidden inside ration bread. When escapes took place, collective punishments were imposed on the whole camp. Although Gruppignano was strictly run by the *Carabinieri*, many prisoners of war preferred this camp to others because it was run efficiently and the 'rackets' which flourished elsewhere were suppressed.[6]

Many inmates considered Vittorio Calcaterra to be a law unto himself, who openly flouted the Geneva Convention; One former prisoner described him as 'a sadist and a beast and an accessory to murder'.[7] Conditions at Campo 57 were extremely harsh: 'Food was poor, and housing was crowded and insanitary. The prisoners had to improvise their own medical treatment, coping with the "57 twins", pneumonia and kidney disease.'[8]

Former POW Australian Lance Corporal Douglas LeFevre, 2/28th Battalion, noted that according to camp folklore there was a notice in Calcaterra's office that read: 'English are accursed but more accursed are the Italians that treat them well.' Describing the atmosphere in the camp, he recalled: 'You could be punished for anything — failing to salute a corporal, punished for smiling or laughing. Italians didn't like to be laughed at, came up with all sorts of punishments, such as making you stand out in the cold, or putting you in solitary confinement, or cutting your hair off — anything to annoy you.'[9]

Prisoners could also be refused hot showers, but possibly this punishment was saved for the winter months. Calcaterra took pleasure in making the men stand for hours on parade, and my father recalled that it wasn't uncommon for a prisoner to faint.

Another report supports this view, listing other so-called misdemeanours:

> For not standing to attention at the lowering or hoisting of the huge Italian flag at the camp gates, for not saluting an Italian officer, for talking during check parade, or for not wearing sufficient clothing near the perimeter fence (apparently considered an incitement to indecent assault) the punishment was 30 days in solitary confinement. Some claim that the commandant kept the cells almost always full as a matter of policy, and that they were emptied to some

> extent only during the visit of a neutral delegate or of a papal representative, or on the occasion of some happy event in the Italian royal family. Nor was brutality discouraged among his subordinates: the camp has a record of handcuffing, 'beating up', and shootings and woundings at least as bad as that at Bari. And although one of the New Zealanders killed there was shot dead while cutting the wire for an escape, another who walked across the tripwire in broad daylight in his pyjamas was obviously at the time mentally unbalanced and could easily have been apprehended.[10]

Some prisoners found the conditions of their confinement impossible to bear, and they cracked. Others played imaginary games. Douglas LeFevre described how some POWs 'used to have a wash and do their hair and smarten themselves up, and they had a piece of string which they would drag along, and they would stop and talk to each other as if they had an imaginary dog'. The guards thought it was daft, but such behaviour helped keep the men sane.[11]

Mason Clark of the 2/43rd Battalion, who also recalled the sign in Calcaterra's office, described him as a 'sadistic, fat little monster'. But perhaps the most succinct summation was that of A. V. W. (Bluey) Rymer, a British wireless operator and air gunner with No. 70 Squadron, who summed up Calcaterra as 'a short-arsed, fat-gutted little shit'.[12]

One small guard named Moronia (nicknamed Twinkletoes) was taught to speak English by the prisoners and played an important role as an interpreter. Perhaps he is the guard in the background of the photograph showing the Allied padre and camp leader outside the building used for distributing Red Cross parcels.

The camp padre and camp leader outside the Red Cross depot at Campo 57, Gruppignano, in 1943. *Alexander Turnbull Library*

There were several solidly constructed communal cookhouses at Gruppignano where food was shared — a vast improvement on the previous camps. However, despite official reports, shortage of food at PG 57 was an ongoing problem. In keeping with the camp's northern location, the prisoners got rice instead of pasta, but the midday soup remained watery. When cabbage became a predominant ingredient, many men suffered from ongoing indigestion, and if lumps of meat were identified, prisoners had bets as to which donkey or horse had visited the knackers' yard.

Again, the prisoners were allowed to supplement their diet by growing vegetables. The seeds were provided by the Red Cross, or the prisoners bought them from their captors, and so animal manure was in hot demand. Cats were allowed to keep down rats and mice, but inevitably in times of hardship some found their way into the cooking pot; faced with ongoing hunger, there was no room for sentimentality. I have been unable to find any record of what the external work camps were like in the Friuli-Venezia Giulia region, but it is likely that here, too, prisoners would have been allocated slightly better rations to carry out their hard labour of 12 hours a day.

Arthur Douglas, who joined Jack's cohort at PG 57 (as did George Lochhead), sketched the New Zealand compound, showing a group of prisoners being closely watched by guards. This work is more sophisticated that some of his Chiavari sketches, for he has included two figures depicted from behind in the foreground, a device used by much earlier painters to draw the viewer into a scene. Douglas may have had access to books on European art at the small library in the camp or he may have learned this device at the art club, one of several instructive groups set up to help prisoners pass the time.

Boxing continued to be a popular sport, as did cricket. Former shop assistant and barman Private Wesley (Wes) Jack (17185) described how a ball was knitted out of Red Cross string and then boiled in

Arthur Douglas's sketch of the New Zealand compound at Campo 57, Gruppignano, made in 1943. *Alexander Turnbull Library*

the cookhouse till it shrank and became rock hard. There were tragic repercussions when an Australian known as Sock Simmons shouted out, 'You stupid bastard, hit the ball!' during a match, and one of the carabinieri shot him, thinking the insult was aimed at him. Simmons died the following day and was given a military funeral.

Such events had a profound effect on others. Wesley Jack stressed how important it was to look out for comrades' mental wellbeing: 'If we saw a man starting to give up, we paid a lot of attention to him, making him wash regularly, and delouse, because if one man failed, the rest would go under.'[13]

As time passed, it became harder for the men to contain their true feelings in letters home. Writing to his young wife Jean in July 1943, former Ōpōtiki share-milker Private Denis Caves (28233) admitted:

> My Own Darling,
>
> Sometimes I realise how unfair we are to ourselves when we write home only reassuring letters of the bright side of our life and leaving out ugly heart-rendering and sordid facts. Many thoughtless ones at home are to think our part easy. They should gain some idea by reading some unvarnished books on the last war. But of course, civilian morale must be kept up — hence lies and more lies. But who gives a damn — those with the power of thought and reason will have understanding. I often wonder if you can imagine what life in a POW camp means after a year and more even to those fit and well and fairly treated. I'm not bemoaning my fate but only on the truth can understanding be built.[14]

According to Italian records, in August 1942 two New Zealand soldiers attempted an escape, but were recaptured after being wounded by machine-gun fire. A group of soldiers then spent a long period planning and digging an underground tunnel, and 19 men got out, only to be recaptured shortly afterwards.[15] The same source is informative about the different work camps to which the prisoners were siphoned, noting the departure of prisoners from Gruppignano to PG 120 camp in Chiesanuova, adjacent to a concentration camp for civilian internees, while on 3 March 1943 a further 50 New Zealanders were sent to Cittadella to work on Gottardo Fratelli's farm. A week later another 60 were sent as agricultural workers to the VIII Work Detachment.[16] There were also work camps at Prati, San Dona di Piave, Torre di Confine and La Salute populated with both New Zealand and South African prisoners.[17]

While there was a regular movement of prisoners in and out of the camp, the Italians had been relatively slow to make use of the vast number of men who could be legally put to work. The Germans had recognised early how prisoners could supplement the dwindling work force at home as more men were enlisted. Official records suggest that Germans were sent to instruct their Italian allies on how to run such camps efficiently, so that when the camps became increasingly overcrowded, siphoning off work gangs was a way of solving two problems at one time.

An advantage for those moving out into the regions was that they could bring back outside news, adding to the information gained via secret short-wave radios built by ingenious prisoners and kept carefully hidden. The discovery of radios in a barracks meant time in solitary confinement, but worse was the destruction of the device so that prisoners with the appropriate skills had to start constructing them all over again.

Campo 57 prisoners, from left: Eric Clark, my father, Steve Oliver, Jim Weston, Jack Duggan and Murray Wylie, photographed while working at the No 2 sub-station. *Jack Arnott archive*

Dad is listed as being at PG 57 from 31 March to 26 July 1943, but he almost certainly spent some of that time at smaller work camps in the region. Another of his photographs shows a line of six men standing in front of a tent in what would appear to be an Italian setting; they are wearing New Zealand dog tags rather than the compulsory rectangular tags issued when they were later transferred to Germany. Dad has identified his comrades on the back: 'Eric Clark, Himself, Steve Oliver, Jim Weston, Jack Duggan, Murray Wylie — No 2, Sub-Station.'[18]

The flat terrain is typical of the Veneto-Friuli plains, rather than the hills and valleys of Pian de Coreglia, and the men's scruffy appearance also suggests that the photograph was taken later in their imprisonment, when their clothes had become more tattered. Dad wears a ragged short-sleeved vest and holds a pickaxe; the man third from right has a brightly polished shovel, indicating he has been using it to dig hard stone rather than softer soil. A slab of marble is at Jack Duggan's feet. Very short haircuts were a way to combat head lice, and the tent behind them suggests they are camping close to where they work.

Back at PG 57, the view on a sunny day would have been charming, the eye drawn across the flat fields to the mountains beyond. One unnamed prisoner evocatively described the differing sensations of camp life: the echoing of church bells ringing out constantly; stamping his feet on the frozen winter mud to try and keep warm; the eternal wait for meals.

He described the play of light from the watchtowers flickering along the wires at night, a constant reminder that he was in prison, and 'the weird solemnity of the funeral processions out to the gate when a man died'. And he referred to the box-like interiors of the huts, the patterns on the walls where he slept, and the strange, coke-like smell of a charcoal burner.[19]

In September 2022, I visited the site of PG 57 with friend and fellow researcher Paula Legel.[20] We took the train from Venice northeast to Udine. Recent rain had refreshed the countryside, and rust-tinted leaves were still on the vines, complemented by fields of grape-red radicchio. Little gardens filled every spare patch of ground beside the railway line, while those too small to cultivate were frothy with weeds. A donkey and two goats watched impassively as our train trundled by, and we could see dustings of snow on the distant Dolomites. It was a far cry from the sepia photographs I had been studying, and I pondered how the colours of the landscape, along with these glimpses of everyday life, affected the morale of prisoners of war.

The following day the driver I had hired through our hotelier arrived at the appointed time and we set out through fields of wheat stubble, some freshly ploughed, under a clear blue sky. Didier Duja — tall, slender, grey haired, his immaculate blue suit perfectly toning with his deep-blue limousine — was charm itself. Like many northern Italians he was polite but reserved, but once he realised I could speak Italian he regaled me with a rapid synopsis of the economy of Udine that seriously stretched my abilities.

He feared the coming winter, as the Russian gas pipeline that had supplied very cheap fuel at 2 euros a measure had been cut and they now had to pay 80 euros a measure to the Americans. He also expressed his distaste for the right-wing movement in Italy, amusing me with that derisive gesture of curling the fingers of his right hand inwards and moving them rapidly back and forth towards his chest.

Although I had been circumspect about giving my reasons for our visit, Didier seemed to understand instinctively that the day held

Above left: Didier Duja, our driver on our visit to PG 57 and PG 103/6, at the end of our day together. **Above right and below:** The front and rear of the chiesetta.

huge meaning for me. Once we arrived at the location of PG 57, he remained in the car, telling me to take my time.[21]

In 1943, the resident camp chaplain, Father Giovanni Cotta, persuaded the commandant that creating a spiritual space within PG 57 would be good for the prisoners' mental health. Described as highly energetic and resourceful, Father Cotta convinced the Vatican to donate the building materials, but the construction was carried out by the prisoners during my father's time and was completed just before the Italian armistice in September.[22] It consists of a simple rectangular hall, fronted by a semicircular porch with rough-cut stone pillars.

My father was not there to witness the opening service, having been moved yet again in July 1943. It was led by Father Cotta, and because it was non-denominational, the Vatican blessed rather than consecrated the chapel. After the war the camp closed, and the chapel fell into disrepair; the roof collapsed and there was major damage to the walls. However, in 1990 the chiesetta was restored by ANGET (Associazione Nazionale Genieri e Trasmettitori, or the National Association of Engineers and Transmitters, Rome), a voluntary military association formed after the war whose aim is to keep alive the sense of solidarity between the military on leave and those in service. I knew nothing of the association when visiting, and I wondered whether the outline of a crest painted on a small shed behind the chapel might have been fascist, and so was relieved to later discover that it was a simplified rendition of the ANGET insignia.

In front of the chapel today there's a stone sculpture of a chained figure, symbolising the misery and cruelty of imprisonment, sentiments also found in the marble plaque that's visible through the locked gates, which refers to the pain and suffering experienced by English, Australian and New Zealand prisoners held at PG 57. I would have liked to enter, because apparently the crucifix above

Above: The crest of ANGET painted on a recently built ablutions block at Gruppignano.
Below: The sculpture in front of the chiesetta.

the altar bears signatures of some of the POWs, but the chapel doors were locked.[23]

I walked across the close-cropped field behind the church to where a glossy chestnut pony was grazing, and I thought of lines from W. H. Auden's 'Musée des Beaux Arts': 'the torturer's horse / Scratches its innocent behind on a tree', unaware of what humanity is capable of.

Little blue butterflies similar to those we get at home fluttered among the stubble, and a persistent horsefly forced me to move further afield, although I knew its irritation was trifling compared to that of the constant lice and flies that had plagued the POWs. Although I was pleased to have finally visited the site of PG 57, I was overwhelmed with grief, for if it is possible for the earth to retain human misery then it does so at Gruppignano. I wept a silent tear for my father, and for all of those who suffered there.

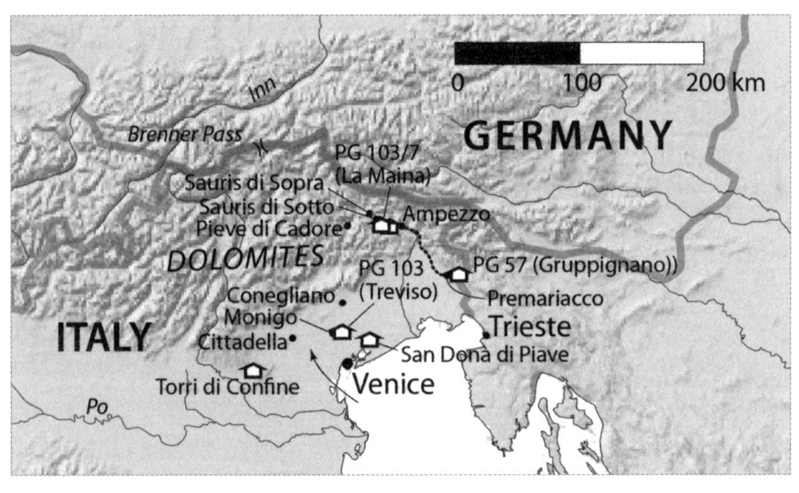

The route of the prisoners' journey in May 1943 from Gruppignano to Ampezzo. *Roger Smith*

12.

PG 103/6, Ampezzo

I discovered the name of the next camp where my father had been held after he died in 1987 and my son and I were clearing out his possessions. Stuck behind one of his drawers was a booklet of drawings printed by Arthur Douglas after the war and sent to all the men who were with him at PG 103/6 Ampezzo. When I mentioned the name to a friend familiar with the Italian alps, they said confidently that Ampezzo refers to Cortina d'Ampezzo. But research is hardly ever straightforward.

Twice in the late 1990s I stayed in Venice for three months, researching for a doctorate (uncompleted), and for economy's sake I lodged in the convent behind the massive baroque church of Santa Maria della Salute at the entrance to the Grand Canal. There were about 20 nuns there, some in their seventies, under the rule of the Bishop of Milan. The other residents were teenage girls who travelled over from the mainland to Dorsoduro every Monday morning to attend university, then returned to their homes for the weekend. The lowest floor was taken up by an asile or kindergarten, the fees providing the revenue necessary to keep the convent running.

For a meagre fee, one of the older nuns kindly gave up her room for the duration of my stay. Its Stark white walls contained two narrow single beds with white coverlets, a desk and a small votive of Christ, who smiled on me benignly. The room was at the end of a long, poorly lit corridor, its window overlooking one of the great volutes atop the drum of the church, and in the silence of the late evening I could hear the slap of water as craft plied the canal, their horns silent due to the hour. In spite of central heating, I felt as if I was living inside an iceberg.

The weekends were solitary: libraries were closed, and the only buildings open were the churches. Vicious winds whipped across the lagoon, making it unpleasant to be out of doors for long, not least because I had only an ankle-length black vinyl raincoat and a fake leopard-skin pillbox hat, très chic in Auckland but entirely unsuited to northern Italian winters. Gradually the nuns became accustomed to my presence, leaving little treats on the shelf outside my door: leftovers from what Artimide the cook had baked for their Sunday lunch (the evening meals served to students were somewhat limited, as the girls were almost always on diets).

Over time, some quietly confided in me their life stories. The oldest nun — the living embodiment of *Whistler's Mother* — crocheted infants' clothing while she sat in a cupboard keeping an eye on the screen that monitored all who entered and exited.[1] It was her window on the world, and I knew I was accepted when the door clicked open as I approached and no longer had to ring the bell. She told me that she had been placed in the convent at birth to make reparation for 'killing' her mother when she was born. Many of the nuns were keen soccer supporters. The most avid among them, a tall nun who would punch the air when a goal was scored, had severe arthritis and found the three flights of stairs very painful, but the bishop refused her request to move to a convent on ground level.

One weekend, I confided in the Mother Superior that I had one day left on my rail pass, and did she think it worth my while to travel to Cortina d'Ampezzo, where I believed my father had been a POW? Minutes later I was heading for the station, changing trains at Conegliano before beginning the gradual climb up into the Dolomites. Eventually, I was the only passenger left, most Italians having more sense than to venture out in what threatened to be a storm. I explained to the charming young guard my reason for travelling, and he got the driver to stop the train briefly while he opened the side door of the carriage and invited me to take photographs down the mist-clad mountain. I was in awe of both the beauty and remoteness of the mountains, and thought how difficult it would have been for prisoners to escape from such country.

The train line finished in Pieve di Cadore, the village where the artist Titian was born. I enquired at the ticket office whether a bus went on to Cortina d'Ampezzo. The woman behind the counter said one did, then added dryly that it only ran on Wednesdays. Without the internet, I had had no way of knowing local bus timetables but, as I discovered later, I was heading for the wrong Ampezzo anyway.

I spent half an hour gathering early wildflowers from beside the railway line, which I pressed in my diary for my mother, made a couple of sketchy watercolours, then boarded the same train for the two-hour journey home. The storm broke overhead, and I got drenched wading through acqua alta. Back at the convent, the nuns whisked my sodden garments away to a vast hot-water cupboard while I regaled them with my day's misadventures.

When I recounted these earlier excursions to Didier as he drove Paula and me on from Gruppignano to Ampezzo in 2022, he chuckled with amusement. The moment we left the bleakness of the plain and started to climb, my spirits rose. The mountains are vertiginous, rocky outcrops projecting out at intervals from patches of scrub or forest. We could see lush pastures in the valleys, but Didier explained that frequent rockslides, some of them serious, account for the variation in vegetation, and he pointed out a village that had been badly damaged by a 6.5 magnitude earthquake in 1976. Though it is now mostly rebuilt, the raw scars of rocks in the distance are a constant reminder of nature's force. Soon we arrived at the village of Ampezzo, where I bought Didier and Paula coffee in a roadhouse. Many of the buildings here are of wood, identical to the kind that scatter Switzerland's hills and valleys, with carved eaves and balconies softened by massed baskets of geraniums. Every blade of grass was carefully manicured. It seemed hard to imagine what the scene might have looked like in 1943.

Another misunderstanding that I had since clarified was the difference between the Monigo concentration camp, which was situated at Treviso, approximately three-quarters of an hour from Venice, and part of which had been designated as Camp 103, and the two subsidiary work camps that are relevant to Dad's history: PG 103/6 at Ampezzo and PG 103/7 at La Maina. The latter was situated about 4 kilometres higher up the Lumiei stream, a subsidiary of the Tagliamento river. George Lochhead had been given the task of organising two groups of prisoners, the first to create a dam at La Maina, and the second to work on the construction of the Lumiei hydroelectric power plant in the Sauris Valley, a project only partially built when the Italian armistice was signed and the camps closed. My father was in the first group of 100 men who moved to Ampezzo on 23 May 1943, a further 108 going up to La Maina a week later.[2]

Many of those transferred to Ampezzo had now been in each other's company for the duration of their imprisonment, and Lochhead must have been fairly certain they would work well together. While there is no record of those who went to La Maina, those at Ampezzo can be clearly identified, because Arthur Douglas's booklet lists almost everyone who was there.

In the introductory page, he describes the camp staff:

> George Lockhead [sic], Camp Leader, possessed of a shrewd ability in dealing with vociferous Italians, George proved himself the right man for the job. It was mainly through his firmness and tact that we were treated as workmen rather than prisoners. Ron McDonald, Quartermaster. 1 between 2 or 3 between 7 — it was all the same to 'Mac'. His fairness and efficiency soon gained him a reputation that he fully maintained later in Kommando 7005, Germany. Lance Johnstone — Cucina. Whether it was macaroni and potatoes, rice and beans, or pasta-asciuta Lance always managed to turn out a tasty brew — sterling work 'Johnny'.

Lochhead was an enterprising man, who in his early days as a prisoner had collated over 500 recipes gathered from various sources, including from former chefs, which he shared with his fellow prisoners. By the time he moved to Ampezzo it had been long confiscated, but he remembered enough to discuss menu possibilities with Johnstone who, with the double rations provided, had more room to be creative. The prisoners were paid a few lire each day, which when pooled would buy them fruit and vegetables from the local Ampezzo market, as well as wine. Cigarettes proved a handy form of currency with the locals.

Unlike at Gruppignano, where Calcaterra took a sadistic pleasure in making the prisoners stand for hours, at Ampezzo morning and evening roll-call was carried out inside the sleeping barracks, just

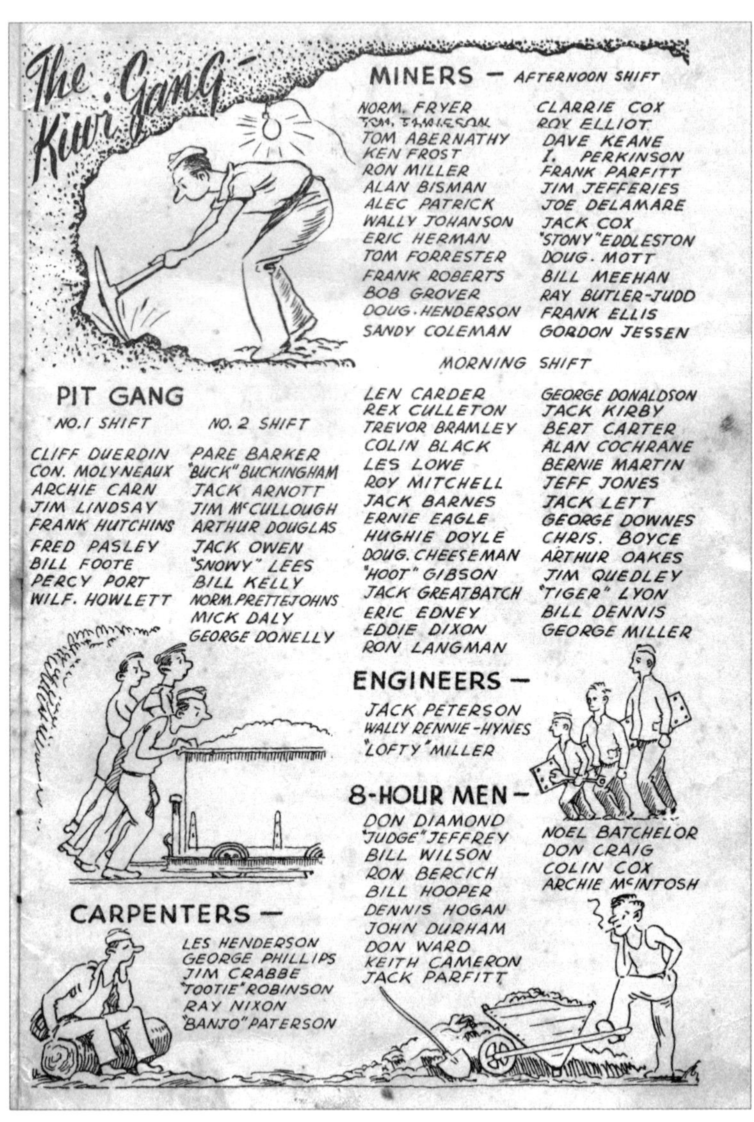

Arthur Douglas's drawings of 'The Kiwi Gang' (above left) and the camp staff (opposite page) in the booklet he published after the war and sent to his fellow prisoners. *Arthur Douglas booklet, Jack Arnott archive*

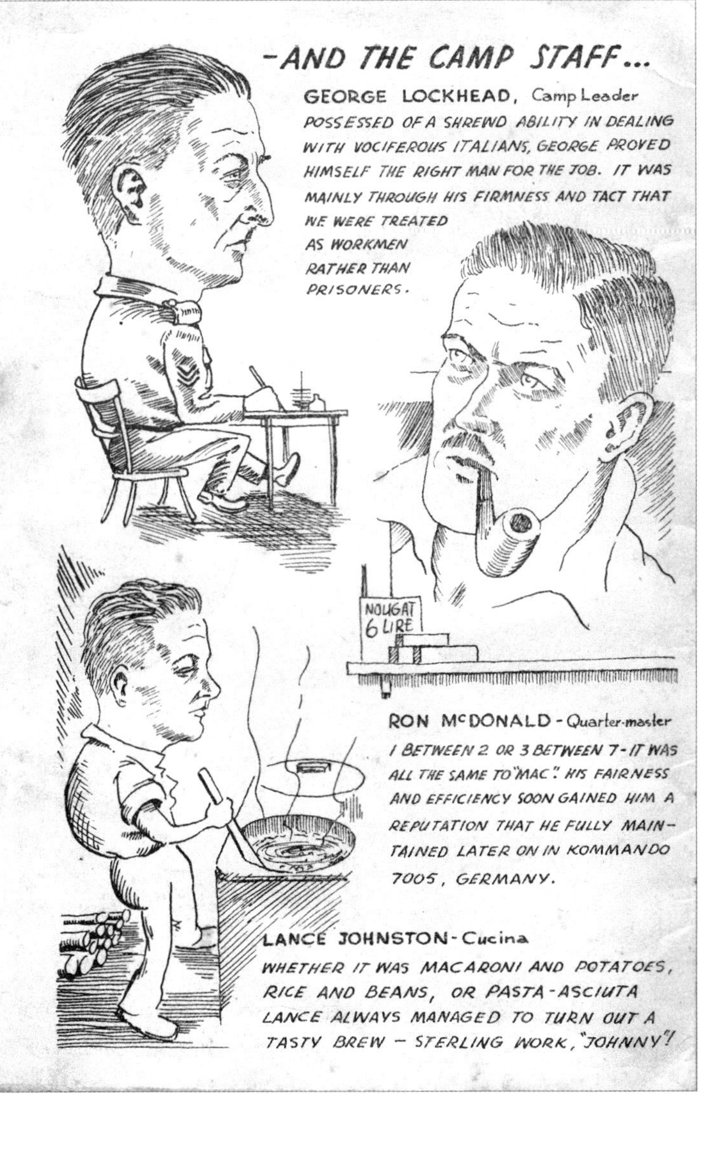
-AND THE CAMP STAFF...
GEORGE LOCKHEAD, Camp Leader
POSSESSED OF A SHREWD ABILITY IN DEALING WITH VOCIFEROUS ITALIANS, GEORGE PROVED HIMSELF THE RIGHT MAN FOR THE JOB. IT WAS MAINLY THROUGH HIS FIRMNESS AND TACT THAT WE WERE TREATED AS WORKMEN RATHER THAN PRISONERS.
NOUGAT 6 LIRE
RON McDONALD - Quarter-master
1 BETWEEN 2 OR 3 BETWEEN 7 - IT WAS ALL THE SAME TO "MAC". HIS FAIRNESS AND EFFICIENCY SOON GAINED HIM A REPUTATION THAT HE FULLY MAINTAINED LATER ON IN KOMMANDO 7005, GERMANY.
LANCE JOHNSTON - Cucina
WHETHER IT WAS MACARONI AND POTATOES, RICE AND BEANS, OR PASTA-ASCIUTA LANCE ALWAYS MANAGED TO TURN OUT A TASTY BREW - STERLING WORK, "JOHNNY"!

as it had been at Chiavari. For humorous effect, Douglas's cartoon suggests a degree of chaos, when in fact a worked-up drawing of the bunks demonstrates a considerable degree of orderliness. The men constructed shelves from spare boxing on which to keep their belongings, and the wooden ledge between the two mattresses on each bunk was a repository for mugs, containers and any personal items such as family photographs. These camps survived on trust, and woe betide the prisoner who tried to help himself to other people's food or belongings. Nails were driven in to hold extra mugs, bags and other equipment, so that personal space, though cramped, was demarcated as a form of 'home'.

Ever diplomatic, Lochhead made it his business to get on with the Italian guards as well as the civilians overseeing the project, always with the welfare of his charges in mind. His job was to select the work parties for each day, including carpenters, engineers, road workers, tunnellers, men to mix concrete, and so on. Dad was in the second shift of the pit gang, whose job was to break up the stone before pushing loaded wagons out to the entrance. The purpose isn't specified, but I presume they were creating the tunnel for water to flow to power the station once the dam above it was completed.

Throughout their years of imprisonment, the men faced a constant difficulty in their boots wearing out. After a standoff with the Italians, Lochhead declared he wouldn't let the men go to work without decent footwear. Ordered to make them work anyway, he advised his men to fill up a barrow, then sit down, take their boots off and empty them as often as possible. The ploy drove the foremen into a fury, and finally the boots were all sent to be repaired.[3]

Arthur Douglas's sketch of the valley at Ampezzo. *Arthur Douglas booklet, Jack Arnott archive*

Frank (Francis) Parfitt (61271), who had been a dredge winchman before the war, is listed in Arthur Douglas's booklet in the miners' morning shift, while his former shop assistant sibling, John (Jack) (7918), belonged to the group known as 'the 8-hour men'. The brothers had lived at home with their mother in Greymouth before serving as gunners in the 14th Light Anti-Aircraft Regiment, New Zealand Artillery. They were both captured in Libya on the same day as my father, and had moved with him from camp to camp, so they knew each other well.

The list is illustrated with a drawing of a prisoner leaning on his barrow enjoying a cigarette, so perhaps this man's job was to fill the wagons that men such as my father pushed. Judging from the sketches, a fair amount of mild sabotage went on, with wagons filled with rubble 'getting away' from the person guiding them. In another sketch a prisoner is about to push a large boulder over a bank, his mate saying, 'Let 'er go now Bert — there's a couple of Ites below!' Sabotage often backfired, and the guards would make the men haul up a rock or a wagon that had 'accidentally' fallen off the track.

Moments of levity aside, memories of the camp could be grim. When Jack Parfitt was interviewed by Megan Hutching for her book *Inside Story*, he recalled his worst moment of the war as the month he spent in the cooler at PG 103/6 after calling a guard a bastard, which the latter took as a literal challenge to his parentage rather than recognising it as a vernacular term of endearment. Jack Parfitt was put to work during the day but spent each night alone in a three-square-metre box with no heating or light and just a tin in the corner as a toilet. At altitude in the Dolomites, even summer nights could drop to 5°C.

Nonetheless, the commandant of Campo 103/6 was generally reasonable, allowing Lochhead to take a group of prisoners for walks in the woods above the camp on a Sunday, with the proviso

Arthur Douglas's drawing of the power station at Ampezzo under construction. *Arthur Douglas booklet, Jack Arnott archive*

that he would be shot if any of his charges escaped. None ever tried. The walks were an opportunity for the men to collect kindling to fuel their blowers for brewing tea should a Red Cross parcel arrive. They also gave Arthur Douglas the freedom to produce some of the landscape sketches that he interspersed among his cartoons.

His landscape drawings are fully worked up, but the sketch of the power station appears to have been done more hurriedly. Indeed, Douglas would have been charged with spying had the commandant known what he was up to. Today the houses in the background have gone; only the power station buildings in the foreground remain.

I had these sketches in mind and was momentarily dismayed when Didier drove past the entrance to the hydro station. He suggested we wait until our return, when he guaranteed all the workers would have gone down to the village for lunch. The site of PG 103/7 was higher up the mountain and reached by several rather claustrophobic tunnels, their walls rough-hewn and dimly lit by eerie orange lamps. According to Didier, the prisoners had helped to cut them out and they were enlarged after the war. We stopped at a vantage point to take photographs of the lake, its vivid turquoise blue complementing the deeper blue of the sky, but Didier was disappointed that recent rainfall meant the spire of the church was no longer visible.

When the power station was finally inaugurated in 1948, the upper valley at La Maina was flooded, and 8 out of the 15 families living in the hamlet lost their homes. Today, Sauris di Sotto and Sauris di Sopra (Lower and Upper Sauris) consist of extremely pretty little houses, clad in plain wood or plastered white, nestled on the hillside. The steep swathe of green mountainside grass is used for grazing in summer, and becomes a piste for skiing in winter, and locals from Udine come to buy local delicacies such as cheese and speck, and to drink the locally brewed beer.

Fat cows grazed contentedly in a small enclosure, and vegetable and flower gardens were scattered here and there. Below the little white church overlooking the lake, the inscription carved on a memorial invoked the locals to live in peace and harmony, and I was drawn to an unusual wooden figure to the right of the gated entrance, topped with what appeared to be a lemon squeezer hat. The POWs may not have been there long, but it seems they have not been forgotten.

We wound back down the hill, and the artful Didier proved to be correct: we swung down the drive to the power station, averting our eyes from the 'no entry' signs and ignoring the CCT cameras on the lower gates. They were open but there wasn't a soul to be seen, the local cuisine having proved too powerful a draw. Through the hurricane-wire fence surrounding the grass-covered roof of the main building I could see the icy bluish-green of the rushing stream, and I realised how accurate Arthur Douglas's drawings were, his lines and shading capturing the denseness of the forest cover, the plunging slopes of the mountains either side and the details of the construction site.

Before visiting the camp sites in Italy, I had never considered the effect of the sounds of nature. The POWs were there from May to September, so during the day the crisp air would have been softened by the warmth of the summer sun. On the plain below, apart from orders from the guards and the conversations of the men, there might have been the odd trill of a bird or the bark of a dog, but in Ampezzo there was a constant rustling of beech leaves and the burbling rush of the Lumiei river as it tumbled down the hillside. The men would hardly have heard this while they were wielding their pickaxes underground or pushing wagons filled with rubble, but in the evenings and on Sundays these sounds would have been ever present.

From top: Lake Sauris, created in the Sauris Valley by the prisoner-built Ampezzo hydroelectric power plant; the memorial at the church at Sauris di Sotto and Sauris di Sopra (Lower and Upper Sauris) showing the lemon-squeezer hat on the sculpture at right; the view down the valley that the prisoners would have had each day.

At the end of summer, however, storms can descend suddenly in the Dolomites, and the region is known for its violent thunder and lightning. Inmates in the camps across the plain below could hear the roaring of the gods in the mountains, accompanied by squalls of lashing rain, but in Ampezzo they would have experienced nature at its wildest. Given my father's love of Otago and its wild weather, I imagined that he would have experienced a similar exhilaration in the Dolomites, and I was comforted that in the middle of their internment he and his fellow New Zealanders had this brief respite, for another kind of storm was about to descend.

The armistice document of 8 September 1943 stated: 'All prisoners or internees of the United Nations to be immediately turned over to the Allied commander-in-chief and none of these may now or at any time be evacuated to Germany.' British Prime Minister Winston Churchill was among those who insisted all POWs be released immediately in the event of an Italian surrender, and that provision would be made to collect them and take them back to Allied locations. He ordered that the condition be inserted in the agreement. But when that decision was quietly overturned, MI9, which was in charge of the original instruction, did not inform him or the war cabinet of its actions.[4]

It is true that logistically, it would have been extremely difficult to deal with a vast number of released prisoners at the same time as the Allies were still trying to secure the country. In the event, it was left to individual camps to decide whether the order to stay put was obeyed or whether the prisoners were given the chance to run.

There was inevitably great bitterness about the British decision to make POWs stay in their camps. Approximately 3700 New Zealanders were in Italy at the time of the armistice, and of these only 339 managed to escape to the Allied lines, while a further 108 made it to Switzerland. A small number were killed while on the run, and eight died while being shipped to Germany. One POW expressed the opinion of many who felt cheated of the freedom for which they had so anxiously waited, politely calling it an enormous blunder.

Ever the ardent fascist, Calcaterra had no qualms about keeping the inmates at Gruppignano locked up, promising they had nothing to fear. Accordingly, a number of them expected British rescuers to throw open the gates at any time. Some men did manage to flee, joining bands of other escapees in hiding throughout the country, often with the help of local people. Almost always it was the poorest who offered them a bed, a meal or a haybarn to sleep in, even though many families suffered terrible retribution for their generosity. The Germans distributed posters warning the Italians of the dire punishments that lay in wait for those who disobeyed orders.

For the POWs who didn't get away, the long and brutish train journey to the camps in Germany lay ahead. In Ampezzo, George Lochhead was tasked with getting the men from both camps down from the mountains. According to Douglas's booklet, 'At 7am on Sept 9th, 1943, we were told "On the Road immediately for Treviso."' Those at La Maina had to move down in such a rush to join the others at Ampezzo that one man left his false teeth in a mug on the windowsill.[5]

My father's cohort, having a little more time, were able to stow their belongings into whatever bags or packs they had. They were to be accompanied by Italian guards who, ironically, were now on the same side, and with whom they shared as many Red Cross parcels as they could, a surplus having been stored in every camp in case of emergencies. The POWs had heard that the British were sending boats to Venice to collect people, and were briefly in a state of high elation, thinking their freedom was close at hand.

Having marched over 24 hours to the railhead at Tarvisio, Lochhead's two groups of prisoners caught the train to PG 103 Treviso, only to find the Germans waiting for them. Lochhead now discovered that he had been promoted to Senior NCO and was to be in charge of 1000 British and 800 Indians, as well as the residents of a Yugoslav internment camp that included women, children and elderly men. Their former guards from Ampezzo were also now prisoners.

The villagers remaining at La Maina had their own problems. The construction of the dam, along with the camp itself, had caused considerable bitterness, one villager recalling that though it had been a pleasure to live there before the war, 'afterwards everything changed. When they decided to build the dam, they couldn't wait to send us away. They took most of the countryside away from us to build shacks for the workers.' An elderly resident recalled their resentment when the fascists made them cut down their forests to make room for the project, and that shots were fired when local partisans tried to stop the dam's construction.

Another added bleakly, 'At the end of October 1948, when the level of the water started to rise, we did not know where to go. When I look at the lake, I know what I have been through and I suffer for this, my heart is down there, I have lost everything, my home, and my fields.'[6]

New Zealand POWs in one of the cattle trucks that took them north to Germany. *Alexander Turnbull Library*

13.

Stalag XI-A, Altengrabow

Where my father had been kept after the march from Ampezzo in September 1943 is unknown — perhaps, like many, he remained in Treviso until finally being entrained north. What is known is that captives were shipped over the Brenner Pass to Moosburg, not far from Munich. George Lochhead insisted on travelling in the guard's truck to ensure that all prisoners received water.[1] Those men owed him a great deal. Conditions were otherwise deplorable. There were no lavatory facilities and each wagon was overcrowded, so prisoners would toss a coin to see whose dixie or mess dish would become the latrine. When full it would be passed over their heads to the one window and its contents flung out. All too often there was a most unpleasant blowback.

Lochhead's promotion would have unfortunate consequences for those who had been in his charge. Once they arrived in Germany, the prisoners were sent to various locations. Lochhead and the other NCOs travelled east to Stalag XX-A at Thorn (Toruń). It was only when Russia advanced into Poland in 1944 that they moved back into

Route of the prisoners' journey in late 1943 from Ampezzo to Treviso, and on to Altengrabow and Fallingbostel in Germany. *Roger Smith*

Germany, to Stalag XI-D/357 at Fallingbostel, near to Stalag XI-B, the final camp at which my father was to be officially listed, although once again much of his time was to be spent further afield in work camps. Meanwhile, he and many other ORs moved to the already overcrowded transit camp at Stalag XI-A at Altengrabow, while still others were sent further afield. The bond that had kept his cohort together had been broken.

Altengrabow lies between Berlin and Magdeburg, in the military district of Hanover. It had served as a prison camp during the First World War before becoming a military barracks in peacetime, its vast array of buildings also including former horse stables. Saplings had been planted in rows when it had housed German troops before the Second World War, but many were stripped by prisoners in desperate need of fuel. Outside the camp stood red-roofed houses for the camp staff; otherwise, a featureless land stretched to the horizon in all directions.

Almost everything I have gleaned about my father's time in Germany has come from external sources, either official or from other prisoners' recollections.[2] It is as if he simply disappeared, and the man who emerged at liberation was a very different being.

Dad was listed at Altengrabow on 15 November 1943.[3] Prisoners' details were recorded on arrival, and their photographs and finger-prints taken. After a medical examination, their head and body hair was shaved for body lice. The men were then issued with a German dog tag made of zinc, indented in the middle so it could be snapped in half if necessary, one part to be buried with the body and the other returned to the Allies as proof of death. My father's is stamped on both halves with Kr-Gef (short for Kriegsgefangenenlager, or prison camp) Stalag XIA and his new German POW number, 158941.

Prisoners working in the snow at Altengrabow. *International Committee of the Red Cross Audiovisual Archives*

Winter was setting in when Dad arrived, and once again bedding proved completely inadequate. The men slept in every garment they owned, no matter how dirty; according to one POW, they all shivered in unison. A former Dutch prisoner, Sergeant Detmar, described how 'the prisoners lay side by side like herrings in a barrel. People slept on sacks filled with paper and if you had to sleep in the main building, you first lay on planks and later on your sacks containing wood wool.'[4]

Unlike at Ampezzo, where all the forced labourers were New Zealanders, in Germany, they found themselves working alongside not only other Allied prisoners but also Polish and Russian civilian slave labourers, who were treated appallingly by their captors. Russia had not signed the Geneva Convention, and the Nazis had no qualms about starving and working these men to death. Allied POWs, distressed by what they saw, endeavoured to smuggle the Russian prisoners any spare food through the wire fences to help keep them alive, but they risked severe punishment if they were caught.

The Dunedin-born printer and war artist John McIndoe (Second Lieutenant, Divisional Supply Column, 9014) was captured on Crete in 1941, and spent the rest of the war in German prison camps.[5] His delicate watercolour 'The Daily Rations of a Prisoner of War in Germany, 25 August 1941' indicates that from early on rations were extremely basic. Without Red Cross parcels, the prisoners would have had little to share.

Inevitably, some took desperate measures. But for those who managed to escape, no matter for how short a time, there were harsh repercussions — a matter of considerable concern to camp leaders who might otherwise be expected to encourage their men to get away. Each time an escape attempt was made, the camps were turned upside down and often all the men punished, even though this was forbidden under the Geneva Convention. As the war ground inexorably on, commandants who heard news of a German POW being mistreated often retaliated by forcing 10 Allied POWs to suffer the same punishment, and reprisals against attempted escapers escalated further.[6]

In March 1944, a secret decree known as Aktion Kugel, or Operation Bullet, enforced summary execution for captured escapees, the bodies to be incinerated to remove evidence.[7] British and American prisoners were initially excluded from this edict, but Hitler threatened to overturn the exemption when it looked as if Germany was going to lose the war. However, knowing that the Allies now held far more German prisoners than previously, he refrained from doing so.

Apart from the main camps (Stammlager) that were spread out across different districts in Germany, there were also sub-camps (Arbeitskommando) linked to them. These could be up to 100 kilometres away, and not necessarily identified by name or number, so it is difficult to identify where my father was working at any time. Prisoners at these work camps would often try to find ways to sabotage the projects they were assigned, little realising that if they were caught they would be sent to a concentration camp at best, or shot as a lesson to others at worst. Although the work was hard, farm labour provided occasional opportunities for scavenging food while a guard was looking elsewhere. Those working in mines or on construction had no such luck. The Germans used explosives

Above: Postcards of the camp at Altengrabow. *Alamy*

to speed up the work in mines, something with which Dad was well familiar, and it is possible that he honed his later skills with explosives at this time.

According to British author and historian Adrian Gilbert, some camp leaders appointed ORs as orderlies to spare them the work camps as well as deprive the German economy of their labour. These leaders had difficult tasks, because ORs were constantly being moved on to different Arbeitskommando, and keeping some kind of order was almost impossible if men snapped under pressure. As in Egypt, the British officers in the camps continued to be conscious of their rank and expected ORs to salute them, but many Kiwis were not about to change their habits despite domineering British warrant officers.[8]

Dad didn't talk about his time in the stalags, although he did teach my brothers to say Scheißhaussen (shit houses), and somewhere along the line he learned German or continental knitting, in which the wool is placed round the needle with the left instead of the right hand, creating a pleasing, slanted stitch. Dad found it easy because he was left-handed; I took to it quickly, too, when he taught me in turn, because I am ambidextrous. What he made I do not know, but many prisoners took up knitting to try to supplement their meagre clothing. Others made embroideries to help pass the time.

Perhaps the most creative example of using apparently innocent materials for retaliatory effect was made by Major Alexis Theodore Casdagli, whose memoir was compiled by his daughter, the artist and actress Penny Casdagli. English, but of Greek heritage, he was captured during the Greek campaign and held in several Oflags (officers' camps) in Germany, and kept a detailed diary throughout that time.

One of his stitched panels, in black and cream, bears the text 'This work was done by Major A T Casdagli, while in captivity at Dossel-

The dog tag issued to my father when he entered Stalag XI-A.
Jack Arnott archive

Above: The daily rations of a prisoner of war in Germany, drawn at Altengrabow by Dunedin prisoner of war and artist John McIndoe in August 1941. *Archives New Zealand* **Below:** Voluntary workers packing next-of-kin parcels in Wellington for New Zealand prisoners of war, 1941. *Alexander Turnball Library*

Warburg Germany December 1941'. The British lion, the Italian eagle, German swastikas and the Russian hammer and sickle are contained in a delicate border, while in the outer border 'FUCKHITLER' is stitched four and a half times in Morse code, while the inner border reads 'GODSAVETHEKING'. When the panel was exhibited in his camp, the Germans never caught on.[9]

He also embroidered a menu for Christmas dinner 1941, as well as numerous bookmarks, exquisite butterflies on patterned backgrounds, and abstract patterns reminiscent of traditional Greek symbols. But the most poignant embroideries are lines adapted from Oscar Wilde's 'The Ballad of Reading Gaol': 'I know not whether wars be right, or whether wars be wrong, all that we know who lie in gaol, is that the wall is strong, and that each day is like a year, a year whose days are long'.[10]

Dividing up turnip peelings from the German mess. Each man is the representative of a barracks of 80 prisoners and stands in front of the cardboard boxes into which each barracks' share is put. *Alexander Turnbull Library*

14.

Stalag XI-B, Fallingbostel

By 13 May 1944, my father had moved to Stalag XI-B, Fallingbostel, in Lower Saxony, northwestern Germany. The camp was very large, housing Anzac POWs, as well as Polish, French, Belgian, Soviet, Italian, British, Yugoslav, American and Canadian prisoners. Two other prison camps were in the immediate vicinity, the sites having been developed in the 1930s when 25 villages between Fallingbostel and Bergen were forced to relocate to create a vast troop training area or Truppenübungsplatz. In the latter part of the war, before being incorporated with Stalag XI-B, Stalag XI-D housed Russian prisoners.

The two parts of the XI-B and XI-D were separated by barbed-wire fencing, and so the Allied prisoners were acutely aware of the appalling conditions in which the Russians were held. Many died of disease or starvation. Stalag 357, which was populated with British non-working NCOs, eventually including some New Zealanders such as George Lochhead, was closed when it was obvious it would be overrun by the Russians. Stalag 357 then became part of the larger

Fallingbostel complex.[1] All through this time, camps in eastern Poland were being emptied as the Russians advanced, but many prisoners did not survive the long march back into Germany.

When news leaked through about the Allied D-Day landings on 6 June 1944, the prisoners were ecstatic, imagining that their release was near. But when it became apparent that this wasn't to be, many fell into despair. Austen Deans, the New Zealand war artist who ended up at Fallingbostel, described how when the running of the camps was taken over by the Schutzstaffel (SS) from 1944, the Austrian guards were afraid to show any sympathy for the prisoners, and conditions in all the camps deteriorated.[2] In Stalag 357, for example, a wash stand that could be used by three or four prisoners at a time had to serve over a thousand men.

Mail deliveries slowed as communication routes took a pounding. The prisoners knew the Allies were advancing but had no idea whether they would still be alive to see freedom. Food consisted mainly of black bread and potatoes so old they earned the nickname of 'mush'. Red Cross parcels were scarce, and supply trucks were frequently targeted by bombers from both sides. By October 1944, the shortage of food had become desperate. Often the midday meal consisted of potato and swede peelings left over from the guards' lunch. A photograph shows a line of men waiting to get their huts' allocation of peel in Stalag 357.

If that was what the NCOs were getting, it cannot have been any better in Stalag XI-B nearby. One former prisoner remembered losing 4 stone (25.4 kilograms) in weight in the last months of the war; others described catching sparrows, and any mangy cat that happened to roam into a camp would be eagerly trapped and dispatched to the pot.

If my father was still at Fallingbostel on 25 August 1944 he would have shared the elation of hearing on the camp radio that Paris had been liberated (the news might have taken longer if he was further afield). But still the war dragged on, although morale lifted in September when Regimental Sergeant Major John Lord marched his 400 crippled and exhausted British paratroopers, who had all been captured at Arnhem in Holland, into Stalag XI-B. The Germans looked incredulously at the immaculate formation of Lord's men, who snapped a salute at the two medical officers looking on in wonder.[3] Appalled by the conditions in XI-B, Lord took over the administration of the camp, determined to improve the morale of the prisoners and remind them they were still military men.

Families in New Zealand were also aware of how grim conditions had become. The New Zealand *Prisoners of War* pamphlet, issued free to next of kin, informed readers of the difficulties in delivering parcels after many of the German railroads had been bombed, as well as the dangers faced by truck drivers attempting to deliver vital supplies to the camps. To ease anxieties, the pamphlet published letters from prisoners in the hope that this would provide solace to families who hadn't received news for some time. Sergeant Edgar Harold (Ted) Everton (31126), an accountant who served with No. 1 New Zealand General Hospital, had been captured in Greece and ended up in Stalag 383. In his letter of 4 November 1944, he thanked his family for writing, and added:

> God knows we need a bit of cheer at this moment. Every confounded thing is short or 'non est' as we used to say. It does not do to dwell on our surroundings nor the displeasure of 14 men in a poky wooden hut for

> another six months of winter. It is more of a mental than a physical misery. We can't get out without getting wet feet.[4]

Over 40,000 prisoners were registered at the complex of camps at Fallingbostel and its outlying work camps.[5] Thanks to *Papers Past* I learned that my father spent some time over the winter of 1944–45 in a small camp near Brunswick (Braunschweig), 110 kilometres by road from Fallingbostel.

An architecturally significant medieval town, Brunswick had been taken over by the Nazis in 1933 and became an important centre for armaments manufacture and headquarters for the military — and later a major target of Allied strikes. When the Oflag 79 POW camp not far from Brunswick was struck by Allied bombers on 24 August 1944, the risk for prison camps that had been deliberately built near munitions factories was clear. Brunswick itself was hammered by the Royal Air Force (RAF) and then the American air force on the nights of 14 and 15 October 1944, and much of the beautiful old city burned for two days. The plan was to destroy enough of Brunswick to make it unliveable, particularly in areas where armaments and aircraft were produced, but the fires that followed left the city a charred wreck.[6]

On the night of 14 October, the RAF feigned an attack on nearby Mannheim, distracting German attention away from the real target so that the city had little defence. The prisoners at Fallingbostel heard the continuous roar as great phalanxes of Allied planes passed overhead on their way to Brunswick. To disrupt radar, strips of tinfoil were dropped before the carpet bombing began, including of old storage tanks, blanketing both the city and the nearby camps in acrid smoke and fumes.

Many citizens had taken shelter in underground bunkers, unaware that they could perish there from lack of oxygen. Quick-thinking firemen created a wall of water which allowed them to get out, but even so a small number suffocated. Those who escaped were confronted with a hell on earth, and it took six days before the fires, fanned by winds that rushed in as hot air rose skyward, were out.

The loss of a city was considered a tragedy, but there was no escape for many of the forced labourers from the east, particularly from Poland, who were without the luxury of refuge in a bunker when the attack began. The bombing failed to obliterate another horror in Brunswick, too. Many of the female slave labourers who had children as the result of rape, either by soldiers or overseers, had their babies taken from them and placed in Ausländerkinder-Pflegestätte (foreign children nurseries), Ostarbeiterkinderpflegestätten (Eastern worker children nurseries) or Säuglingsheim (baby homes), where they were deliberately starved to death.

George McMurtry, a captain in the Wiltshire Guard, described how dangerous Brunswick's location was even before the main raid took place:

> It had a flying bomb site on one side and there were tank works on another side in an airport, so it had all these targets around it. And we got used to having the British coming over at night and their Mosquitoes and they seemed to let the bombs go before they got to the camp. They'd go over the top of us and then bomb targets on the other side. It was May so they knew they were there; they were very accurate and never hit us. By contrast, the Americans in their flying fortresses coming over by day hit us and killed one or two prisoners.

McMurtry also reported on the perils of attempting escape as guards turned dogs on fugitives whenever they had the chance. Not all Germans were brutes, and there are accounts of kindness shown to prisoners in extremis, but this was the exception rather than the norm.[7] Major Harry Sell's outrage at German brutality and misconduct is manifest in his account of time spent at a camp in the locality, with one particular incident making a lasting impression: 'I have a private score to settle with one Gfr. Rebun for blowing out the brains of a Gurkha Officer in Brunswick just for the fun of it.'[8] Sell's record of life in his camp later provided vital evidence in securing the conviction of Oberst von Strehle, the Commandant at Brunswick, for ill treatment of prisoners.

In the face of SS brutality, New Zealander J. Barber took direct action on the farm where he had been sent to work alongside other POWs and civilian slave labour, striking a guard who had been beating Polish children. Barber only narrowly escaped execution; by chance, the German army, which had a record of ill feeling towards the SS and the Gestapo, ran the court-martial that dealt with him. After the war, the Polish ambassador praised Barber for his brave stand.[9]

If many German guards displayed appalling brutality to their prisoners, they were obsessed with the wellbeing of their dogs, having been ordered in 1942 to rush their charges to the nearest vet if they showed any sign of ill health or change in their behaviour. After one dog leapt from a moving train and disappeared into the night, an order was placed for all troops to look out for it so it could be returned to its master. The contrast with the treatment meted out on a vast scale to Jews and other so-called enemies of the state could not be more stark.[10] In 1944 a sub-camp of the concentration camp Neuengamme was constructed in the vicinity of Brunswick. Here Jewish prisoners lived and very often died in appalling conditions.

During the particularly grim winter of 1944, my father's work gang was tasked with rebuilding the damaged railways at Brunswick, working for 12 hours a day and being paid a daily rate of one German mark. The work was gruelling: the ground was frozen to a depth of a metre, and the men's clothing was grossly inadequate for the conditions.[11] For months after the raid, the smell of charred buildings lingered in the air, and the Germans were in no mood to treat Allied POWs well. Perhaps huts were provided for the workers, or they may have slept in local barns, but many local citizens also needed housing, so the options would have been limited.

NCOs were rarely given permission to accompany ORs when they were moved to German work camps, depriving prisoners of one of their few protections against abuses and adding to their sense of isolation and vulnerability. Despising Christianity and other organised religions, the Nazis also tried to stop Allied padres from visiting the work camps, but many padres insisted it was their right according to the Geneva Convention and were ultimately issued special passes to do so.[12]

By the end of 1944, the Allies were continuing to pound Germany, and Red Cross trucks continued to try to find new routes to reach the camps, knowing that many prisoners were on the brink of starvation. It could take eight months for a family parcel to come through, and by the new year deliveries came to a halt. In these dire circumstances, imagination and talent broke the monotony, with music in particular an antidote to depression. Reading was important, too, and when the weather was fine there were football matches between the different nationalities. And at last news that the Allies were making real progress could be learned via the prisoners' secret radios. Reports were then spread through the camps, a glimmer of hope for the men who had been incarcerated for so long.

Every night the prisoners could hear the thundering of Allied bombers flying over Germany, and those who had to trek through the snow to the latrines may well have seen them too. Hitler developed an obsession with Allied pilots, declaring that because the planes were causing such destruction, all airmen in prison camps would be forced to remain behind to rebuild Germany. But as New Zealand Infantry Corporal Charles Watkins (46177) sardonically noted, when the war was won Hitler wouldn't be in a position to declare anything.[13] After British intelligence got wind of Hitler's declaration, leaflets written in German were promptly dropped all over German territory:

> ALLIED PRISONERS OF WAR WARNING TO ALL
> IN CHARGE OF THEIR WELL-BEING.
>
> The government of Great Britain, the American government and the government of the Soviet Union direct here in the name of the nations at war with Germany, a warning to all commanders and guards who have authority over allied prisoners of war in Germany or German occupied territory, as well as to members of the Gestapo and to all other persons regardless of whatever branch of service or whatever rank who have in hand Allied prisoners of war, be it in the combat area, lines of communication, or air area, they declare herewith that all those persons and the German high command, all Army, Navy and Air Force commanders are held personally responsible for the security and well-being of those under their command. Anyone who mistreats Allied Prisoners of War or who allows such mistreatment regardless as to whether in combat, lines of communication, camp, military hospital, in prison or wherever, will be hunted down and punished. This responsibility is binding under all circumstances and cannot be transferred to any other authority or person. Signed: Winston Churchill, Harry S Truman, Josef Stalin.[14]

Finally, the end was in sight. In March 1945, a month before liberation, a batch of Red Cross parcels that had been held in store in Lubeck arrived at Fallingbostel, saving many prisoners from dying of starvation. They did not have long to wait. As in Italy, the prisoners were ordered to stay where they were until their liberators arrived, but most were too weak, in any case, to make a dash for freedom. Still, it was a nervous time. A week or so before liberation, the section of Fallingbostel that held air force POWs was told it had to evacuate, while those who remained were concerned by posters hastily put up by the Germans calling the Russians the real enemy: 'England will find herself isolated against a Soviet Europe and Soviet Asia from the Atlantic to the Pacific.'[15] It was a message that created equal anxiety among families at home.

My father was back in Fallingbostel when American forces took the town on the morning of 16 April 1945, overthrowing its Nazi government, while the tanks of the 8th King's Royal Irish Hussars, a British armoured regiment, rolled into sight and the gates at the adjoining camps at Fallingbostel were thrown open. It was a remarkable sight. In XI-B, cheering prisoners clung to the wires as the Hussars approached, and at the main gate of Stalag 357 the inimitable R. S. M. Lord and his group of paratroopers were among those lined up to greet their liberators. The degree of malnutrition among the captives was immediately apparent. A photograph of British prisoners shows them sitting shirtless on the ground in the spring sunshine.[16] They are skin and bone — but they are free.

Another reckoning was due. Many prisoners had sensed what was happening in the extermination camps. Airman Bob Johncock, who

British POWs after their release from Stalag XI-B, Fallingbostel. *United States Holocaust Memorial Museum, courtesy Eric Fenton*

grew up in New Zealand but served with the RAF and later the Royal New Zealand Air Force (RNZAF), recalled seeing 'the trainloads of victims obviously heading for these places. It was also common knowledge in Germany that this went on, but the average person in the street was too frightened to admit it.' Posters suggesting that Hitler was listening were displayed in every town and village; even the walls had ears. Johncock noted that local children were deterred from misbehaving with the warning: 'If you don't play properly, you'll go up the chimney.'[17] As a result, most local people turned a blind eye to the reality of the concentration camps: it wasn't their problem. Viktor E. Frankel, a survivor of Auschwitz, recalled the relief felt by Jews if they were moved to a camp that didn't have a chimney: they knew they were safe for now.[18]

As the American troops moved north, gradually liberating POW and concentration camps, nothing could have prepared them for the shock of what they saw. American war correspondent Helen Kirkpatrick, who was following the troops closely, wrote:

> I spoke to one of the emaciated looking group who'd been force marched from their POW camp alongside the retreating German army and had been allowed nothing to eat beyond the scraps of animal feed they could forage on their way. Their treatment had been in blatant violation of the Geneva Convention, and it inspired new levels of hatred among the active soldiers. Some of the American conscripts had come reluctantly to this war, regarding it as an abstract issue, a quarrel over alien soil.

Now all they cared about was defeating the Germans, and she noticed how rarely they even spoke to their families about what they were witnessing: 'Death, dirt and weariness are the familiar . . . it is impossible for them to think of a world of baths and home-cooked food when everything within eye range is broken and spoiled.'[19]

In Stalag 357, George Lochhead had been working as an assistant in the morgue and had become acquainted with a doctor who visited Bergen-Belsen concentration camp after its liberation by the Allies. This was the camp where the young diarist Anne Frank and her sister had died of typhus the year before. On his return to Fallingbostel, the doctor told Lochhead, 'That's the smell we've been smelling. It's from there. We hadn't known what the horrible smell was. It was only fifteen kilometres away.'[20] The men in the other camps around Fallingbostel knew this smell too.

The BBC's Richard Dimbleby accompanied British troops into Bergen-Belsen:

> Here over an acre of ground lay dead and dying people. You could not see which was which . . . The living lay with their heads against the corpses and around them moved the awful, ghostly procession of emaciated, aimless people, with nothing to do and with no hope of life, unable to move out of your way, unable to look at the terrible sights around them . . . Babies had been born here, tiny, wizened things that could not live . . . A mother, driven mad, screamed at a British sentry to give her milk for her child, and thrust the tiny mite into his arms, then ran off, crying terribly. He opened the bundle and found the baby had been dead for days. This day at Belsen was the most horrible of my life.[21]

In 1965, a set of memorial gates and a memorial plaque were erected at Bergen-Belsen, representing the gateway through which 17,000 emaciated prisoners from 13 nations had finally walked to their freedom.

15.

Repatriation

From the camps, the released prisoners were sent to a transit centre in Brussels, where they queued according to nationality before being flown to England. My father was photographed in front of a Dakota aeroplane wearing an American parachutist's jacket, his cinched belt indicating the weight he had lost during his time in Germany. His only possessions seem to be the bundle of papers stuffed in his pocket.

Fortunately for Dad and the thousands like him, army attitudes to the repatriation of prisoners of war had improved since the Italian armistice in 1943, when a report drawn up by the New Zealand Section of the Allied Repatriation Unit in Italy had stated, among other things:

> Any ex-prisoner arriving in our hands should be treated as a normal soldier who has returned to duty after having had a *slack* time. He should be first 'processed,' clothed, and documented and receive information on military matters to get him up to date, and his liability to Army orders made

My father stands in front of a Dakota transport plane at an airfield in Brussels in April 1945, before being flown to England. *Jack Arnott archive*

> clear so that there is no doubt if he makes any breach of orders he should be punished for breaches as a normal soldier . . . Special treatment, leave or concessions such as UK leave on a big scale should be avoided.[1]

In the interim, the effects of long-term imprisonment on a soldier's physical condition and his state of mind had become better understood.

The logistics of managing around 8400 New Zealand Army former prisoners of war had to be carefully thought through. Some authorities suspected that the men would rebel against harsh treatment after their experiences in the camps, and that any criticism would be reinforced by families at home who felt their sons had sacrificed enough. To avoid confusion, families had been informed of how mass repatriation was to be organised even before prisoners left German soil.[2]

Once the POWs arrived in England, the *Waikato Times* was among the newspapers that published reports setting out what this entailed, including recuperation in first-class hotels on the English south coast. For the duration, these hotels were renamed wings, each accommodating 50 officers and 1000 men. Now a major-general, Howard Kippenberger was convalescing from a war injury in England, and took on the role overseeing this complicated process.

Puttick Wing (in civilian life the Wingcliffe Hotel), served as the initial reception or transit camp at Cliftonville, Margate, where all ex-prisoners were processed before being sent to their selected recuperation wings. By the end of April around 100 officers and 1100 other ranks had been received, of whom a substantial number had been processed and were already on leave. They were issued with new uniforms, reinforcing that they still belonged to the NZEF, and given appropriate dental and medical treatment. The marked effects

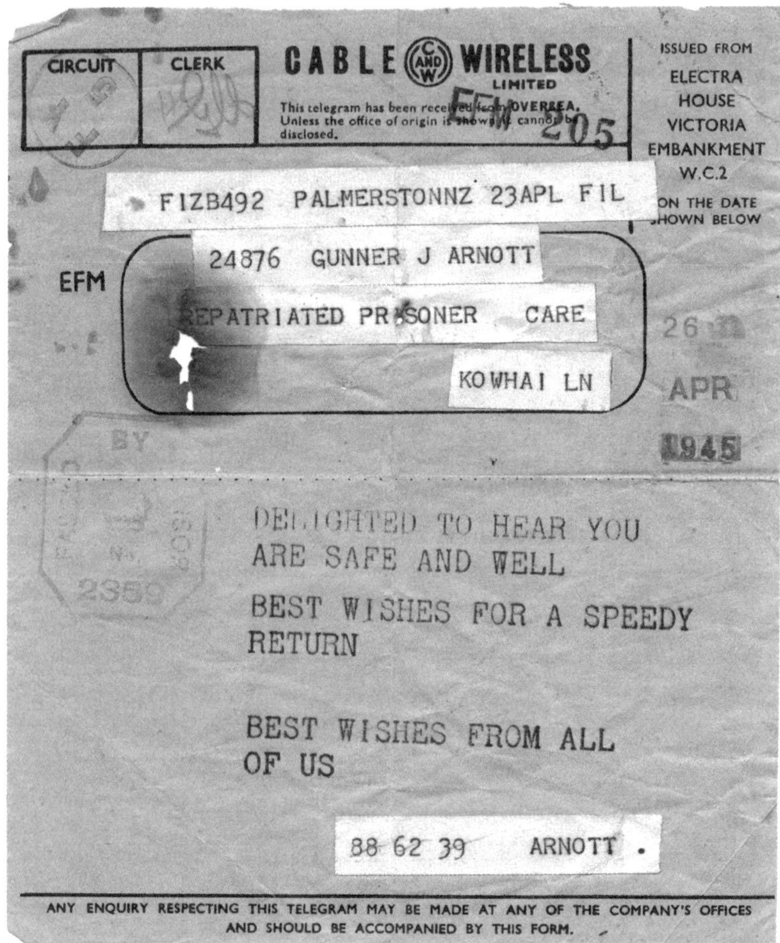

CIRCUIT | CLERK

CABLE AND WIRELESS LIMITED

This telegram has been received from OVERSEA. Unless the office of origin is shown it cannot be disclosed.

EFM 205

ISSUED FROM ELECTRA HOUSE VICTORIA EMBANKMENT W.C.2 ON THE DATE SHOWN BELOW

FIZB492 PALMERSTONNZ 23APL FIL

EFM

24876 GUNNER J ARNOTT

REPATRIATED PRISONER CARE

KOWHAI LN

26 APR 1945

DELIGHTED TO HEAR YOU ARE SAFE AND WELL

BEST WISHES FOR A SPEEDY RETURN

BEST WISHES FROM ALL OF US

88 62 39 ARNOTT .

ANY ENQUIRY RESPECTING THIS TELEGRAM MAY BE MADE AT ANY OF THE COMPANY'S OFFICES AND SHOULD BE ACCOMPANIED BY THIS FORM.

My grandmother Frances Arnott's telegram to Jack. *Jack Arnott archive* of lack of food and the long marches were immediately apparent, and about 250 of the first tranche of POWs were admitted to Haine Hospital.[3] An unexpected side-effect of the now plentiful food was the rebellion of shrunken stomachs, exacerbated if too much alcohol was consumed.[4] My father seemed in relatively good physical condition, apart from his weight loss, and unlike many had managed to hang on to his upper denture.

Each prisoner had to answer a range of questions about their individual experiences in the camps, including whether they had ever tried to escape, cause sabotage in any way or had collaborated with the enemy. The army was particularly eager for evidence of war crimes by their captors, and there was a separate form to record whether the Geneva Convention had been flouted. Once these details had been taken, a cable was sent to inform families in New Zealand of the safety of their loved ones. When Dad's mother Frances received notification that Jack was safe and well, she immediately replied, selecting the approved phrases numbered 88 (Delighted to hear you are safe and well); 62 (Best wishes for a speedy return); and 39 (Best wishes from all of us).

Dad and other New Zealanders who had trained in the North Island were directed to the Freyberg Wing in Folkestone, which was located at either the Grand Hotel or its neighbour, the Metropole, both highly desirable summer residences in peacetime.[5] The town is steeped in the history of both world wars. Among the vast number of men and women who sailed from Folkestone to France in the First World War was the doomed poet Wilfred Owen, who described the Metropole as a 'place of luxury . . . with carpets as deep as the mud . . .'[6]

A reply to this telegram may be sent from any branch of Cable and Wireless Limited, the addresses of which will be found in the Telephone Directory, or from any Postal Telegraph Office, using up to three of the following texts, for a charge of 2s. 6d. for a complete message.

CORRESPONDENCE

1. Letter received many thanks
2. Letters received many thanks
3. Telegram received many thanks
4. Parcel received many thanks
5. Parcels received many thanks
6. Letters and parcels received many thanks
7. Letter and telegram received many thanks
8. Telegram and parcels received many thanks
9. Letters sent
10. Parcels sent
11. Letters and parcels sent
12. Many thanks for letter
13. Many thanks for parcel
14. Many thanks for telegram
15. No news of you for some time
16. Writing
17. Urgent
18. Please write or telegraph
19. Please write
20. Please telegraph
21. Please reply worried
22. Airgraph letter received many thanks
23. Letters arriving regularly
24. Have you received letters
25. Your letters not received
144. Please address letters home
145. Have you received telegram
146. No parcel for some time
147. Write same address
148. Parcel sent
149. Writing regularly
150. Your parcels not received
151. Have you received parcel

GREETINGS

26. Greetings
27. Loving greetings
28. Fondest greetings
29. Love
30. Darling
31. All my love
32. All my love dearest
33. All our love
34. Fondest love
35. Fondest love darling
36. Best wishes
37. Greetings from us all
38. Loving greetings from all of us
39. Best wishes from all of us
40. Fondest wishes from all of us
41. Best wishes and good health
42. Kisses
43. Love and kisses
44. Fondest love and kisses
45. Well
46. All well at home
47. Best wishes for Chr[illegible]
48. Best wishes for Chris[illegible] and New Year
49. Loving wishes for [illegible]stmas
50. Loving wishes for Christmas and New Year
51. Loving Christmas thoughts
52. Happy Christmas
53. Happy Christmas and New Year
54. Good luck
55. Keep smiling
56. My thoughts are with you
57. Many happy returns
58. Birthday greetings
59. Loving birthday greetings
60. Happy anniversary
61. You are more than ever in my thoughts at this time
62. Best wishes for a speedy return
63. Good show keep it up
64. Best wishes for [illegible]w Year
65. May God grant you a year of happiness
66. God bless you and keep you safe
67. My thoughts and prayers are ever with you
152. Love and best wishes for New Year to all at home
153. Best love from daddy
154. God be with you till we meet again
155. God bless you
156. Love to daddy
157. My love and greetings on Mother's Day
158. My love and greetings on Father's Day

HEALTH

68. Family all well
69. All well children evacuated
70. All well children returned home
71. All well and safe
72. Are you all right
73. Are you all right worried about you
74. Please don't worry
75. Hope you are improving
76. Please telegraph that you are well
77. Are you ill
78. Have you been ill
79. Illness is not serious
80. Illness is serious
81. I have left hospital
82. In bad health
83. Health improving
84. Health fully restored
85. Son born
86. Daughter born
87. Am well and fit
88. Delighted to hear you are safe and well
89. So glad to hear that you are better
90. Have not been ill
159. Hope you will soon be better
160. Have not been well
161. Injury is not serious
162. Anxiety unnecessary
163. Going into hospital
164. Operation over condition satisfactory
165. Hope children all well
166. Both well
167. Twins born
168. How are all the family
169. Injury is serious
170. I am in hospital

PROMOTION

91. Congratulations on your promotion
92. Very pleased to hear of your promotion
93. Delighted hear about your promotion
94. Have been promoted
95. Have been decorated
96. Have received commission
97. Congratulations on your commission

MONEY

98. Please send me £X
99. Please send me $X
100. Have sent you £X
101. Have sent you $X
Note.—The actual amount in words to be inserted immediately after the text number.
102. Can you send me any money
103. Glad if you could send some money
104. Have received money
105. Have you received money
106. Have you sent money
107. Thanks for money received
108. Have not received money
109. Unable to send money
110. Sorry cannot send money
111. Do you need money
112. Have paid £X into your banking account (amount to be inserted)
113. I do not need money
114. Can you make me daily allotment
171. Have sent money
172. Can you increase the allotment
173. Are you receiving allotment
174. Business very bad grateful financial assistance
175. Expect to be able to send you money next pay day

CONGRATULATIONS

115. Congratulations on anniversary best wishes
116. Congratulations lasting happiness to you both
117. Glad and proud to hear of your decoration everybody thrilled
118. Loving greetings and congratulations
119. Good luck keep it up
120. I wish we were together on this special occasion all my best wishes for a speedy reunion
121. Very pleased to hear you have passed examination
122. Best wishes to all at home
123. Our thoughts are with you
124. Love to all the family

WAR DAMAGE

125. X . . . injured and in hospital
Note.—The name to be inserted immediately after the text number
126. Injured and in hospital
127. Sorry to hear of damage hope all well
128. Sorry to hear of injury and hope not serious
129. Sorry to hear of injury and hope progress favourable
130. Sorry to hear of injury and hope soon be better

MISCELLANEOUS

131. What things do you need most urgently
132. Have done as you asked
133. Rumour not true
134. No
135. Very happy to hear from you dearest am fit and well
136. Hearing your voice on the wireless gave me a wonderful thrill
137. Hope to see you soon
138. Hope
139. Your telegram not received
140. Yes

176.xFather
177.xMother
178.xWife
179.xFiancee
These can be inserted in front of items numbered X hereunder

180. X . . . writing telegraphing frequently
181. X . . . writing weekly
182. X . . . writing regularly, receiving no reply
183. X . . . anxious welfare, no news recently
184. X . . . receiving letters regularly
185. X . . . receiving letters occasionally
186. X . . . well, receiving allotment
187. X . . . recovered operation returning home
188. X . . . is entering hospital
189. Hope to broadcast greetings from BBC listen X
(X—day of week to be added by filer)

BEREAVEMENT

141. Sorry to tell you X . . . died
142. Sorry to hear X . . . died
Note.—The name to be inserted immediately after the text number
143. The Lord bless and sustain you in your loss

HEAD OFFICE OF THE COMPANY : ELECTRA HOUSE, VICTORIA EMBANKMENT, LONDON, W.C.2.

Telegraphic Address: EMPIREGRAM, ESTRAND, LONDON — **Telephone: TEMple Bar 1222**

The official form from which Frances selected the sanctioned phrases for her telegram. *Jack Arnott archive*

Situated on the Leas, the promenade running along the clifftop at the western end of the Folkestone seafront, the Metropole and the Grand provide magnificent views across the English Channel to France when the weather is clear. The Metropole, which was taken over by the war department in October 1939, acted as a records depot and then as a field dressing station. Winston Churchill stayed there occasionally during the war, when sick or injured Allied soldiers were stationed in the wards on the lower floors, and both buildings had developed hospital facilities, including a small operating theatre, in the basement.[7]

When I visited Folkestone in 2022, the Metropole had been converted into luxury flats, and it was only by waylaying a returning jogger that I managed to wangle my way inside the building, causing the concierge some consternation until I reassured him of my purpose. He then became extremely helpful, inviting me to take any photographs I wanted and showing me a copy of a little book that recorded the building's history. He also showed me a photograph of a smiling woman astride her courier motorbike; the Metropole had been used as a drafting depot for women about to serve in France in the First World War.

Today, new blue and gold carpets are a colourful contrast to the elegant, flecked-marble columns in the foyers that lead the eye up to handsome coffered ceilings. Victorian murals of Romantic themes in the style of Edward Burne-Jones grace the shallow lunettes above the walls, and the foyer is illuminated by glittering chandeliers. After the filth and deprivation of the prison camps, arriving in such surroundings must have been a surreal experience.

The neighbouring Grand Hotel was built to compete with the Metropole, using more modern building materials and techniques. In 1909, King Edward VII and Queen Alexandra opened its new dance floor, and the King also enjoyed the hotel's comforts with

The Grand and Metropole hotels, Folkestone, in 1945. *Jack Arnott archive*

his mistress, the vivacious minor aristocrat Alice Keppel, who now has a bar named after her.[8] Agatha Christie, tapping away at her typewriter at a dining table overlooking the sea during the 1920s, wrote some of her best-known novels here, including *Murder on the Orient Express*.[9] The hotel was also immortalised in the script of Noël Coward's *Blithe Spirit*.[10] In its time, it was an exciting place to be. On the ground floor the famous Palm Court restaurant remains, its glass walls and roof allowing diners to enjoy the views without being battered by the winds coming off the Channel. Sadly, I had less success getting into the Grand than the Metropole, as I was unable to afford the £200 (approximately NZ$415) cost of a high tea.

The centre of town, which still retains some very handsome Regency buildings, lies in a kind of amphitheatre sloping down to the harbour. During the Second World War, that part of the south coast between Folkestone and Ramsgate, including Dover, was nicknamed Hellfire Corner, a title originally given to the highly dangerous Menin Road in Ypres in the First World War. The towns along the Sussex coast once again took the brunt of powerful guns the Germans had transported up the railway line from Calais after the capitulation of France in 1940.

In Folkestone, more than a hundred severely damaged properties were surrounded with empty lots full of rubble, including the site of the gasworks. When the last of the batteries at Cap Gris-Nez was captured by the Canadians on 30 September 1944, the church bells in Folkestone rang out, heralding that evacuated families could safely return to their stricken town.

All along the south coast, children, often without the company of their mothers, had been evacuated to South Wales and Monmouthshire to escape danger. However, stalwarts like my own mother-in-law Alice, having initially been made to move with two young children, returned to sit out the war in Eastbourne. People got used to VI flying bombs (known colloquially as doodlebugs) whistling overhead, accompanied by the constant drone of aircraft on their way to bomb cities further north. Many fell short of the mark, and 45 doodlebugs intended for London killed three people and seriously injured 24 others in Folkestone alone.[11] The English Channel was littered with wrecked ships and downed fighter planes, and few local fishermen could continue working, but many of them ignored the danger of mines and went out to rescue Allied airmen who had bailed out or come down in the Channel.

For the POWs, reminders of the war were everywhere on this coast. Most of the zigzagging paths leading down the cliff were closed off, and the beach was still covered in rolls of barbed wire, although cranes were gradually burying it under the sand. The town also bristled with barbed wire, and in the front gardens of the Metropole tarpaulined guns faced the sea. The section known as East Cliff Sands had re-opened to the public, however, and there was a café where you could buy tea and enjoy soft drinks near the lapping sea.[12] It was a strange world, and to smell the sea air and know that you were no longer in danger was initially hard to come to terms with.

To ease their repatriation, local papers encouraged locals to take returned POWs into their homes and show them the same hospitality they hoped their own boys still fighting in the Pacific would one day receive. One can only admire a community that, in spite of its own experiences of grief, loss and financial hardship, would open its doors to returned prisoners.

The welfare side of the repatriation organisation had also been carefully considered by the military, including the establishment of a residential club in London staffed by the New Zealand Women's Army Auxiliary Corps. My father's paybook notes that he was allocated backpay to the sum of £39.10.8d in three instalments between 18 and 25 April — a fortune for someone who hadn't handled real money for three and a half years. The book reveals that he was on leave in London on 8 May for the jubilant Victory in Europe Day celebrations, and that he took the opportunity to visit Windsor Castle as part of the organised tours offered to ex-POWs. He may also have taken advantage of the free rail passes that allowed all ex-POWs to travel further afield. He did not return to Folkestone until 28 May, by which time he had been paid out £135.0.8d. Some of this may have been paid directly into a New Zealand bank account, as officials began to worry that the men would squander all their accumulated pay rather than saving it for their return to New Zealand.[13]

I wandered the town, visiting the Folkestone Museum whose excellent displays provide a treasure-trove of historical and contemporary information. The Folkestone Library is tired by comparison, its water-stained walls much in need of refurbishment, and from the corner where I perched between a photocopier and a printer I observed a long line of desiccated wasp corpses lying on a ledge. Even so, the helpful librarian provided me with envelopes of newspaper cuttings from the Second World War, along with various booklets full of invaluable information, all of which made me wheeze from their years of accumulated dust.

In April 1945 the local newspaper, the *Folkestone, Hythe and District Herald*, published detailed interviews with British returned POWs, who reported on the terrible conditions in Germany, the lack of food, the long marches during which many died of exhaustion, and the brutality with which they had been treated. Returnees also talked about the overcrowding and unsanitary facilities in the camps.

As a result, officials gained important insights into the psychological effects of ongoing imprisonment. A report for the Psychiatric Division of the British War Office was drawn up:

> Other things being equal, the difficulties of social readaptation on repatriation appear to be more severe in ex-prisoners of war than in any other body of men so far studied . . . Emotional problems are disproportionately severe in men who have been prisoners for more than eighteen months . . . Planning the rehabilitation of these men demands particular care — Not soft handling, but different handling.[14]

Some of the ex-POWs were asked if they were prepared to talk in depth about their experiences so that doctors could get a better idea of how stress and loss of freedom had affected them psychologically.[15] Their reactions differed widely. When interviewed for the *Free Lance* in New Zealand, Ted Everton said, 'It's odd getting used to freedom. Here at the reception-camp we've been given everything we could possibly wish for except one thing, a cure for our restlessness.'[16] For many long-term Allied prisoners like my father, the reality of freedom was hard to grasp.

English Lance Corporal Tony Vercoe was overwhelmed by everyday life: 'Outside, I felt a hint of hesitation. This was Britain and here began the world, true freedom, normality. How to deal with it?'[17] Others felt disconnected from the world they had known before the war. Feeling he should celebrate, Sergeant Pilot Jack Rae went to one of his favourite London pubs but found that it was filled with strangers.[18] Many preferred spending their free time on their own — sitting in a corner of a pub with a pint or going for walks, not wanting to engage in conversation. Some experiences were still too raw to be talked about.

New Zealand's director-general of medical services had made the decision that men would be patched up physically in England and then, when ready, returned to New Zealand and civilian life as quickly as possible. There, it was hoped, time and the company of understanding families would take care of any anxiety. Several senior officials in New Zealand, concerned that people would make too much fuss over returning prisoners' states of mind, advised that it would be better for families and loved ones not to ask about their experiences. That POWs could be suffering from conditions akin to post-traumatic stress disorder was little understood.

16.

The return home

New Zealand's former POWs had weeks at sea during which to consider what life would be like at home. When Lieutenant-General Sir Bernard Freyberg addressed the New Zealand forces who had continued to fight for the duration of the war in Italy in February 1945, he recognised the difficulties many would face on their return. He praised their magnificent efforts, acknowledging both the failures and triumphs, perceptively adding:

> I venture to think we shall look back with the greatest pride to the times when we fought without adequate equipment. It was then that our Star shone brightest, then that our best work was done, holding the enemy in the Middle East until the Allies were organised on a war footing. Greece, Crete, Sidi Rezegh, Minqar Qa'im and Ruweisat Ridge are names which will be amongst our proudest memories.
>
> On going back to civil life all of us ought to make at least one resolution, that is that we take an interest in the affairs of ex-servicemen. I hope that you will all join your local

> Returned Services' Association and do all you can for those ex-servicemen who find it difficult to become settled again in civil life.[1]

However, the return home failed to eradicate many POWs' underlying sense of shame, and they kept their experiences to themselves. Sergeant Major Jack Elworthy of the 16th Light Aid Detachment, New Zealand Ordnance Corps (22820), who was imprisoned in Lamsdorf, Poland, before moving to Germany, recalled a British air force man whose face had been badly scarred after he jumped out of his burning plane. He had received a balaclava, a scarf and a pair of gloves from a well-wisher in England, but when he wrote to thank her, she replied that she meant them for a live fighting hero, not for a coward who gave himself up.

Another British prisoner was told in a letter from his fiancée that she was breaking off their engagement because she would rather marry a ''44 hero than a '43 coward'.[2] Similar attitudes to returned POWs were recorded in Australia. Australian historian Christina Twomey's postwar study of POWs notes that some prisoners were reluctant to seek financial assistance because it would add to the feeling of disgrace that was a consequence of their time in prison camps.

Despite Freyberg's advice, some New Zealand POWs found they weren't welcome at their local Returned Servicemen's Association branch because they were regarded as cowards. Some joined the rival Ex-POWs Association, set up by the New Zealand Army in an attempt to combat such prejudice. Articles published in its newspaper *POW WOW* were intended specifically to educate the population about the real experiences of being a prisoner of war. Rejecting the notion that captivity was dishonourable, Kippenberger also exhorted POWs to have pride in what they had endured and overcome: 'In every camp they bore up against adversity, defied and deceived their guards, maintained discipline, soldierly spirit, and pride of race. Only a very few failed.'[3]

Later, writers such as military historian Chris Pugsley have noted this sensitivity to shame and failure, but have argued that there is little evidence the ex-POWs were viewed as shameful by the general public.[4] Nonetheless, I remember being told by a boy whose father was a fellow soldier that my father was a coward, and for years I quietly worried that it might have been true.

There were also difficulties between reunited couples. Australian returned POW Russell Braddon later wrote:

> There seemed to be this wall of almost wilful incomprehension. Subsequently we learned that the medical experts had advised our family and friends when we got back not to encourage us to talk about it, to steer us away from it . . . we would start talking about what had happened and instantly people were busy changing the subject, looking bored as all hell. They were in fact agitated, thinking you were going to go off your nut.[5]

Inevitably, many returned prisoners felt their experiences had not been of value to society. If you had been captured early on in the war, you could make no contribution to discussions about battles and manoeuvres, and it didn't help that by the time prisoners landed back on home soil they had gained enough weight for there to be little evidence of the constant deprivation they had endured in the camps.

Private Jack Gallichan (45933) encountered a similar difficulty when reproducing the *Tiki Times*, the prisoner-run newspaper that was written and circulated at a working camp in Poland. Its republication in 1950 was designed to take casual readers into the life of a POW work camp, but it could never take them into POWs' hearts, where only supreme optimism could crowd out the hopelessness and bitterness of a life full of hunger and scheming, of longing and hope, and of resignation to the overlordship of a brutish foe.[6] Regardless, *POW WOW* made a determined effort to keep the experiences of returned POWs alive over the coming years. At a reunion event for the association, the deputy mayor of Hamilton opened proceedings by acknowledging: 'There is no way that I and other members of my generation can really understand what you went through.'[7]

Another underlying bitterness arose because the Ex-POW Association argued that prisoners should receive some compensation for the years they had been incarcerated, particularly those who had been forced into labour like my father, and those who hadn't received their due in Red Cross parcels. The government said it would look into the matter, but no recompense eventuated.

Unlike members of the RSA, many ex-POWs didn't wear medals — not because they hadn't earned them but because, as one former soldier put it, they knew too much about war. My father was a case in point. He was persuaded to write away for his medals only two years before he died.

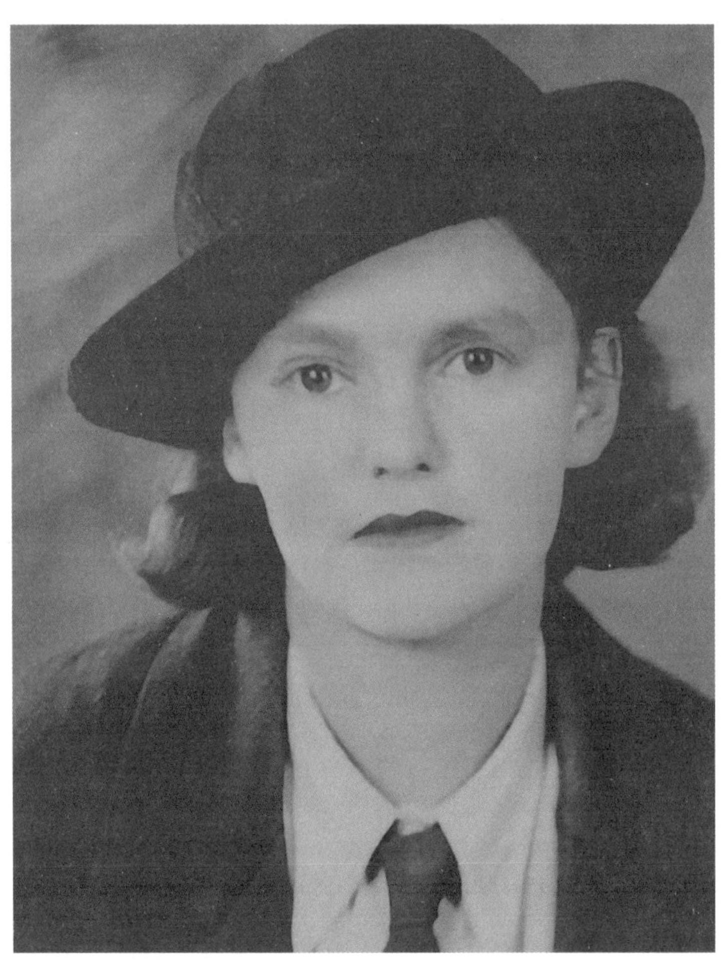

My mother, around 1939.

17.

Aftermath

Strangely enough, I now know more about my father's experiences during wartime than about how my mother filled those years. She and her younger sister Winifred remained living at home at 27 Landscape Road with their parents for the duration of the war. In this hand-coloured photograph from about 1939, Ethelwyn's sombre outfit reflects the clothing restrictions introduced once the war began, her white shirt and dark tie suggesting a woman ready to do a man's job, which wasn't quite the case.

At the time the New Zealand Division was engaged in the Battle of Sidi Rezegh at the end of 1941, Ethelwyn received a letter inviting her to volunteer as a nurse overseas. She promptly wrote to her parents to tell them the news. They were staying at Te Whanga in Whangaparāoa with old family friends, the Shakespears. My grandfather, after discussing the letter with them, wrote back to Ethelwyn advising her not to take up the offer, as her poor health would make her of little use to the armed services. Once again my mother was made to feel inadequate, and she turned down the offer to volunteer.

My grandmother Emma had become seriously ill, having been initially misdiagnosed as suffering from hysteria. Years later,

Ethelwyn remained bitter that it was only when doctors finally operated that they found a cancerous tumour that had grown too large to remove. The stress of nursing Emma until she died in 1943 caused the return of the bouts of stomach troubles that had given Ethelwyn's family so much concern, but my mother recovered. Now that she was no longer needed at home, she was taken on as a voluntary nurse aide (VAD) at the Auckland Teachers' Training College buildings in Owens Road, Auckland, which had been turned into a nursing home for soldiers invalided home from the war.

A photograph, since lost, showed Mum in her uniform with other nurses beside several men who were sitting in wheelchairs or were supported by crutches. She and the other volunteers received very little training and were expected to use common sense and 'get on with it'. She recalled being constantly anxious that she would do something wrong and harm her already damaged patients. However, what she could offer was a kindly ear, her gentle manner making her popular with the patients. (I didn't inherit her patience, but I can still make a bed with impeccable hospital corners.)

My mother told me once that during the war she had been in love with a man named Pat, who served in a ski patrol on the Swiss border. After she died, I found several photographs in her crocodile-skin writing case showing distant, white-uniformed figures skiing below a line of pine trees. In the end, she said, marriage to Pat was out of the question because she didn't share his Catholic faith.

Her talented sister Win had missed out on attending university because in the Depression of the 1930s my grandfather could not afford the fees. As an accountant he had work, but his income dwindled considerably as many clients found themselves unable to pay him. Instead, Win attended secretarial school and worked as a shorthand typist at Prestige Millinery, possibly becoming responsible for my mother's lifelong passion for frothy headgear.

At the outbreak of war, Win had enlisted with the Women's Auxiliary Army Corps (WAAC), joining the civilian staff at the Auckland Army Headquarters, Area 1, Drill Hall, in Rutland Street. The work was mundane at first and involved sitting all day typing lists of names for rolls and forms. Eventually Win's shorthand skills were put to better use in the major's office. This proved far more stimulating, not least when she was initiated into the procedure of courts of inquiry, including doing the typing for a court-martial, which she described as 'complicated'.[1]

Life took a sadder turn for both sisters when in late 1944 their father also became ill. With his daughters working, he returned to Ellamore in Mount Eden to be nursed by his three sisters, and he died shortly before the war ended. Win had been closer to her mother, but Ethelwyn adored her father, and every time she talked about him when I was young, a wistful look would come over her face.

On 7 July 1945, the personal column of the *Otago Daily Times* referred to my father's return to Otago:

> Gunner Jack Arnott, of Palmerston, who returned to his home recently after being a prisoner-of-war in Germany for three and a half years, has been visiting Milton this week in company with his mother, Mrs W. Arnott. Gunner Arnott was a popular member of the Toko Football Club while resident in Milton, and he expressed thanks to the secretary of the club (Mr H. Wilkinson) for the club's generous donation towards a parcel . . .[2]

If Dad had a tūrangawaewae, Milton was it. However, after a brief spell with his family, he returned to Auckland and re-established contact with my mother. This suggests they had remained in touch, although she never mentioned writing to him while he was away. My instinct is that he would have sought her out, and she would have been glad he did. Jack Arnott seemed to offer a chance of happiness and the family she had always longed for.

When I asked my mother years later why she had married Dad, she answered, 'Because he could fix things'. It brought to mind the story she told about how she and Dad went on an outing to Auckland's west coast beaches with family and friends, and the vehicle they were travelling in broke down. While the other men in the party threw their hands in the air, my father set to and fixed the engine so that they could resume their journey.

During their two-month engagement they were photographed at 27 Landscape Road, sitting together in the sun. Glued to Dad's side, my mother is holding a large tabby cat, which rests its head on Dad's arm, while he in turn holds its paw. They were married at St Barnabas Anglican Church in Mount Eden on 29 September 1945. The wedding was simple, but despite ongoing restrictions on fabric, my mother wore a snappy tailored suit with a scalloped front, and a rakish hat with a rose in a style that was the rage at the time, and which may have been provided by her sister.

Shortly afterwards, my parents moved to Dunedin. My father longed to be nearer his mother, in a community where he was known, and where he had earned respect before the war. They moved into a small flat in York Place, up from the Octagon, but it wasn't long before Ethelwyn found Dunedin difficult — she was lonely, knew no one, and apparently their landlady was a terror. Worse, there were already signs that her marriage was not going to be easy. Like so many returned POWs, Dad had recurring nightmares, and she would

Above: My parents, Margaret Ethelwyn Gray and Jack Arnott, during their engagement, in Auckland in August 1945. **Left:** My mother on her wedding day in September 1945.

wake at night to find him gone, striding the streets of Dunedin in the dark, unable to cope with being confined. She conceived almost immediately, in spite of earlier warnings from doctors that she might be unable to have children, and she finally persuaded my father that they should return to Auckland where she would have the support of her family. They moved back to live with Win at 27 Landscape Road.

My brother John was born on 11 August 1946. His birth was very difficult, for my mother was tiny, and she was bedridden for three months. Dad briefly hired a nurse to look after her until Win generously agreed to leave the army in September to take on the role of carer — a duty still expected of unmarried women at the time. A year later my parents bought number 37, the bungalow in which my great-grandmother had lived, three doors down the hill, taking on a mortgage that was paid out only 10 years before my father's retirement.

No doubt my mother took comfort that many of the neighbours she had known from childhood were still living nearby, some in the elegant and very substantial houses that sat atop the hill, and number 37 and its large garden, although not her childhood home, were full of family memories. The two-bedroom bungalow was small, and my mother later claimed that it was saved from falling down because the borer were holding hands.

On 16 August 1947, two months before I was born, my father was permanently discharged from the army (NZ822 Certificate of Discharge 39503). I arrived the day they moved into number 37, and when my mother said she needed to get to the hospital, my father, thinking she was fussing, asked her to wait until he had finished hanging the curtains. It was Labour Day; they got caught up in race-day traffic, and only just made it in time. At birth I weighed 4 pounds 10 ounces (under 2 kilograms); when they took me home, Dad put me in a shoe box to see if I would fit.

Although my father doesn't appear to have had a girlfriend back at home during the years of his long incarceration, the notion that women were fickle, unfaithful and not to be trusted was a tool used in German and Japanese propaganda to unsettle Allied prisoners, suggesting that while they were suffering in prison their wives and sweethearts were being seduced by Americans who plied them with silk stockings and other luxuries. Indeed, many women had a wonderful time with the 'Yanks', who seemed more courtly and charming than so many young New Zealand men.

Dad was only too familiar with the insults that Bill Arnott had flung at Frances during his childhood, and now mistrust started to grow within him too. The irony of this is painful: my mother was terrified of intimacy, not least because she became pregnant so readily. My younger brother was born 11 months after me, and she feared she would have a child every year till she died.

I could have been no more than five or six years old when my father borrowed money from one of my mother's aunts to buy the lease on a quarry at Whatawhata, outside Hamilton, on the banks of the Waipā River.[3] Like many other ex-POWs, he was happiest when he was on his own, and he would spend the next few years there, apart from brief visits home. I remember visiting there once, more excited about a baby lamb he had borrowed from a neighbouring farmer for me to play with than paying attention to the tiny hut in which he lived. It was fairly primitive, by all accounts (I remember only a dark, unpainted wooden interior), but it was his to do with as he pleased. My older brother has clearer memories, because he was once sent to stay with Dad for a fortnight one school holiday. The land was prone to flooding and, stranded, they survived on a loaf of mouldy bread and pūkeko soup. How Dad caught the bird is not recorded, but John said they were hungry and it had to suffice.

In spite of his need to be alone, Jack missed company, and he took to driving his truck to a nearby town to visit one of my mother's cousins, a worldly, headstrong woman of independent means who proved all too keen to provide my father with the physical affection he felt was lacking in his marriage. The affair came to an end when, after another flood, he was forced to abandon the quarry and return to Auckland in 1954. He was never able to repay my great-aunt, who accepted that the debt would have to be cancelled. Her own husband had been badly injured before being captured in the First World War, and perhaps she had some insight into the troubled mind of an ex-POW.

Two of Mum's siblings owned baches at Murrays Bay on Auckland's North Shore, where they spent their summer holidays. They knew the area well because the family had had a hut by the stream on Mairangi Bay until the Labour government confiscated it for the homeless after the war. Wanting to give us seaside summer holidays in the company of our cousins, most years my mother managed to save enough money for us to rent accommodation of our own.

The first I remember was a primitive little bach that she rented one year when I was about five. It had the advantage of being next to the substantial fibrolite bach built by her younger brother Howard when he came back from the war, and we were in awe of its large sitting room and modern cane furniture with coloured bands of green and red, as well as of its large windows looking out over the sea, so different from the dark stained wood and somewhat gloomy interior of Landscape Road.

Our little bach was extremely rudimentary. The lavatory was outside in the garden: a tin can in a hut draped with cobwebs in which spiders lurked. We would watch out for the night-cart man, who rumbled up the road in his truck every week before striding up the garden with an empty can balanced on his shoulder. He would emerge with a full, stinking can, hoist it onto his shoulder and stride down the path again, leaving a pungent odour behind him. My father, of course, was impervious to such things, having experienced much worse overseas. And if the can was unpleasant, at least there was no danger of falling into it — my ongoing fear when using the more traditional long drops found in many baches.

That year, my father travelled up from Whatawhata, arriving at the bach late on Christmas Eve, long after my mother had tucked us into bed. He had been given a bottle of whisky as a Christmas present — a gift we all came to fear — and the inevitable row ensued. On Christmas morning I discovered that my presents had been damaged. Dad had wrenched the blonde wig off a little doll my mother had saved up to buy, and a miniature tin cooking set had been crushed. Mum said he only did it to hurt her, but I was heartbroken. If my uncle had overheard the row, he obeyed the social dictum that you didn't interfere with other people's marriages. My mother began to feel that my father had a split personality, and that his gentle and violent sides were irreconcilable.

Yet there were also many happy times at Murrays Bay. We roamed the local beaches, and in a photograph showing a mob of cousins and parents sitting on the sand Dad is in the front row beside me, his hand resting on my ankle. That was the year Dad encouraged me to jump with him off the long wooden wharf that stretched out into the bay. He hadn't considered our different body weights, and I was dragged down deeper and deeper, my hand clutched firmly by his, struggling to hold my breath. Often, in the evenings, we would gather in one of the baches and sing, accompanied by a honky-tonk piano, ukulele and the ubiquitous tea-chest. Many of the songs were from the war, and all the adults knew them by heart.

We knew from my mother that Bill Arnott wasn't Dad's real father, and that he had treated Dad very badly as a child, and so my brothers and I were not inclined to like him. He and Frances came to stay only once, when I was about eight years old, and Michael and I had to move out of our bedroom to accommodate them. Bill, tall and lanky in a navy pinstripe suit, treated us with evident disdain, and we liked him even less after he kicked our cat. Aspects of our family life may have been rambunctious, but *nobody* was allowed to kick the cat. The boys didn't help matters when they kicked a football through our bedroom window, shattering the glass.[4]

My mother fretted because according to Dad Frances was a superb cook who could knock out a batch of feather-light scones on her coal range, while Mum's own attempts were often better suited for target practice. I'm sad I have no other memories of Frances, because I know that she loved my father and had always defended him when Bill's rages got the better of him.

My mother was a reluctant cook who mistrusted food, but she would faithfully copy out recipes into a notebook with a worn pencil in the hope that she could replicate them. My father would mock her efforts when he really wanted to upset her. He had a very good arm, on one occasion hurling his plate from the new red Formica dining table (my mother's pride and joy) in the sun porch. It went through the kitchen and landed with a crash against the front door, fortunately missing the mottled glass panes at the top. A mass of tired mince and shards of white china slid gradually down the door to the floor. If he had come home at the normal time instead of drinking in the pub, the meal wouldn't have been so dry.

The kitchen at Landscape Road was at the heart of the house, narrow, with a green enamel stove at one end of a rough green and cream terrazzo bench, and an icebox at the other. When we were little we watched in fascination as thc iceman carried in the large block of ice on his shoulder, protected by a sheet of hessian, before lowering it carefully into the box with the aid of an iron hook.

Once the austerity of the postwar years had passed, Mum bought a refrigerator on tick, and a wringer washing machine to replace the large copper in the washhouse, which each day she'd have to fire up before feeding the wet laundry through a mangle set up over the concrete tubs. Such purchases could land her in financial trouble, not least if Dad came home in a bad mood on pay day, having spent more than he should have in the pub. Many men sought out each other's company in the bars when they first returned from the war, but too much alcohol only exacerbated my father's condition. When his mood turned nasty, he would go into the public bar and pick a fight. On the occasions when he refused to give Mum all the housekeeping money, we children were called upon to help her decide which bill she should pay first.

I was seven when, to help make ends meet, my mother took in our first lodger, a beautiful but extremely deaf young woman from a farm in Kumeū, who was now working in the city. Her name was Addie. Mike moved out of our room so she could share it with me, and we all came to adore her. When she married her farmer sweetheart, I was her flower girl. It was the kind of wedding my mother had always dreamed of, with long frothy dresses and shiny black cars that delivered us in style to St Matthew-in-the-City. I asked Addie years later if she had been bothered by the tensions in our house, and she laughed, saying she just used to take her hearing aids out.

There was another woman in my father's life whom we all loved equally, and that was his sister, Jean. It may have been she who told my mother about my father's difficult childhood. We got to know her family well when we spent a fortnight with them in Tauranga one school holiday. Goodness knows how they fitted us in, as their house was small, and Jean and Frank had several children of their own. Possibly we topped and tailed, as children often had to in those days. Frank was a butcher, and my cousins delighted in taking us to the local abattoir, seemingly impervious to the horrors we glimpsed through a gap in the wall as a great black beast was dispatched before tumbling down a ramp to the slaughtermen below. The image played in my nightmares for months afterwards.

At the end of our holiday, we took the train back to Auckland, and while we were on the bus home we saw Dad's truck driving into town. He had mistaken the time of our arrival, and my mother fretted, understanding how badly he wanted to be there to greet us.

Dad continued working as a quarryman, eventually becoming quarry manager at Ihumātao, excavating stone for Auckland's new airport. The farmer who had acquired the site was unaware that the hill they were demolishing was an ancient part of the isthmus with Māori connections over centuries and an archaeological treasure trove. Quarry work is always hard, but Dad loved the rolling fields and old stone walls at Māngere, and the light playing across the surface of the Manukau Harbour, which turned murky grey when the wind whipped up. He would take us floundering at French Bay in Titirangi, or to collect cockles, which he would cook over a sheet of corrugated iron.

He also became a relative expert on the use of explosives.[5] My mother drew the line at dynamite, but he did bring home boxes of gelignite when he had a job to go to first thing, and one Guy Fawkes night he let us run round the back garden waving gelignite flares, their flames shooting out in front of us into the darkness.

My mother talked to me frequently about her life before she was married, as well as alluding in oblique terms to what we sometimes experienced at home, as if by speaking what she knew out loud she would somehow make sense of it all. Possibly as a result of her Quaker background, she despised the use of physical violence. She felt it demonstrated weakness, lowering the individual to the level of an animal who reacted by instinct rather than controlling anger through reason and intellect.

One might wonder what kept my parents together. Certainly, my mother and I once visited a solicitor who, having ascertained that she had no independent means of support or skills, told her she couldn't afford the luxury of a divorce, and we took the bus home again. But there were things my parents shared, not least their pride in us children, for in spite of his behaviour under stress there is no doubt that Dad loved us.

As children, we had never had the luxury of store-bought clothes, relying instead on hand-me-downs from my mother's wealthier friends, and I can clearly remember Dad getting out a razor blade to cut the toes out of a pair of worn red leather shoes when they became too tight for me to wear. Near the end of intermediate school, a dance was organised by the teachers. The girls had to make their own dresses in sewing class, and my parents bought me my first pair of new shoes — oyster-coloured satin pumps with ribbons, impractical for day wear but deliciously soft to wear. We had to have our first dance with our fathers, and it was a dreamlike experience as he lightly whirled me round the floor.

By the time we were teenagers, bedrooms had been added on to the house and my mother was able to move into my old bedroom. Dad excavated a space under the house to create a room for my brothers, which was accessed through the washhouse, which remained a gloomy, cobweb-hung space with old blue bags mouldering away on the wall nogs. Unlike the boys' room, my new bedroom was a proper one, built by a carpenter who extended our sitting room at the same time, but to reach it I had to cross the back porch. At night, conscious of the dark garden stretching down out of sight, I was always relieved if the bathroom light had been left on, the window casting a speckled brightness that made me feel secure.

My mother was a highly sensitive, warm-hearted woman who was always trying to help people — once even sending my older brother onto a neighbour's roof to cover her chimney with wire after a possum had dropped in uninvited. At different times cousins came to board so that they could be closer to grammar school or university. One fondly recalled my mother as a delightful, somewhat absent-minded woman who provided a friendly home for her family, and our old cat, who kept Patrick, our large mongrel dog, in awe. His younger sister believes that even though my mother hadn't lived up to the academic standards of her family, she became its emotional heart, someone in whom everyone confided and whom they turned to for advice.

We became more independent as we got older, my brothers becoming ardent sports players with a wide circle of friends, and in our teenage years we often left our mother to her own devices, not that she ever remonstrated with us. I took to staying at a friend's house, irritating my family who teased me by calling me by my friend's surname. My father remained unpredictable, and tensions continued to seesaw at home, but the periods between outbursts gradually lengthened.

We were one of the first local families to get a black-and-white television, and my brothers' friends, boys from the First XV or First XI at Auckland Grammar, would come over to watch their favourite programmes. They were somewhat on edge, sensing the atmosphere in the house and later describing my father as a 'hard man', but the lure of television overrode any unease. Television also became a form of escapism for my father, even if he did once kick it.

In spite of his rages, my father had never hit us. Then one day when I was a recalcitrant teenager who demanded to be allowed out with my brothers, he knocked me across the kitchen into the fridge door. I was too stunned to be aware of pain, and he was appalled at what he had done. Instead of leaving the house, I sat with him at the kitchen table while he talked about his childhood and the war, trying to explain why he was driven to such lengths.

In my late teens, I became pregnant, something my mother kept from my father, fearful of his reaction. She must have confided in her own family, because the autocratic Waikato cousin demanded that I have an abortion, while the latter's sister wanted my mother horsewhipped for failing to educate me about contraception. I, on the other hand, was determined to keep the baby. Having little understanding of the ramifications, like so many pregnant teenagers, I felt that if I had a child I would have something to love.

After one family meeting at which I was told I couldn't get married because the father-to-be was a Catholic, I tearfully walked for miles

My father and me at my wedding. *Bruce Cavell*

around Auckland before finally ringing home. My father answered and, on hearing the strain in my voice, said simply, 'I don't care what you've done. Come home and I'll look after you.' And true to his word, when it became obvious that the only way I could keep the baby was to get married, my parents did everything they could to help us. We would marry in a Catholic church, but my fiancé insisted that the baby would not have to be brought up in his faith.

My mother was adamant that I should have a proper wedding dress, and chose a seamstress at Māngere Bridge, far enough from home to be discreet. A friend from school agreed to be my bridesmaid. The morning of the wedding my father took my fiancé to the pub. I never learned what Dad said to him, but I can hazard a guess that it involved a warning of what he would do to him if he ever hurt me.

When the sleek black car arrived to take us to the church, Dad was kindness itself, making sure that my veil didn't fly off in the wind. At the back of the church, he rested his hand over mine briefly before walking me down the aisle. It was a typical shotgun wedding; my mother almost fainted and my younger brother sobbed quietly. I was blithely unaware of how my pregnancy had affected others, but a photograph taken outside the church by a friend of my husband's suggests that I had broken my father's heart.

Later, one of my uncles said I should return all the wedding presents as we had got married under false pretences. As an 18-year-old mother-to-be, I had little use for a silver tray and crystal whisky glasses, but I kept them anyway. In a similar vein, the day after my son was born at National Women's Hospital, the Waikato cousin left a marzipan mouse for me at the hospital reception, possibly implying that I was still a child in her eyes. The following evening, my father and brothers, who were desperate to see me and the new addition to the family, hired dress suits and, breaking the 'husbands only' visiting rule, charmed their way in past the matron on duty to come to see me and my baby. I had been feeling particularly wretched, and I nearly cried when they burst into the ward with grins on their faces.

I would not have survived the next 18 months without the support of my parents. Dad became a very loving grandfather, although I did warn him once that if he ever got drunk in front of my son, he would never see him again. Right from the start I had difficulty in feeding the baby because he didn't suckle. My mother persuaded me to stop breastfeeding, but he then suffered from projectile vomiting and I discovered he was allergic to cow's milk.

After one particularly bad night when I had given him five bottles in a row only for him to vomit profusely after each of them, I rang my mother and said that if she didn't come over I was going to throw the baby out the window. She replied that I was to put the kettle on and she would get the bus immediately. On other occasions Dad would come over in his car, and we would lie the baby on the back seat and drive him round and round till he fell asleep.

Inevitably, my marriage didn't last. Again, without my parents' help, I would have found the next two years almost impossible. When my son was three I began training to be a primary school teacher. Students were paid to train then, and the lecturers, knowing I had a small child at home, let me do my artwork in my little flat and attend classes in person once a week. I loved it, for in those days we were taught philosophy, drama and modern literature alongside traditional subjects, and I was eager to learn. I was also delighted to make new friends who didn't mind at all that I was a young mother.

There were some droll moments. I had started seeing my future husband David, who while studying at university had got a holiday job labouring on the construction of an extension to Rocklands Hall, the Auckland Teachers' College student hostel in Epsom. His supervisor had kept saying that 'Big Jack' was coming to 'pop the rocks' but David had no idea who he was talking about.

A few days later, I was passing on the bus to teachers' college when I saw Dad's old Chev going up the drive to the hall. Although Dad had met David a couple of times, asking darkly 'Who's the girl?' because of the length of David's hair on their first meeting, we had tried to downplay the extent of our relationship. I rang my mother in a panic to tell her David was working there. She said quietly, 'He'll probably kill him.' That day it was David's turn on tea duty, and as he rounded the corner with a tray, tea towel foppishly draped over his arm like an English dandy, he ran slap bang into my father. The foreman then told David that he would be my father's assistant for the day and was somewhat bemused by a certain frostiness that descended at his words. Dad growled at him to get a slab of steel out of the boot of the Chev (David could barely drag it), which they would use to cover the drill holes in which gelignite was placed. He then told David to stand on it.

In spite of everything, by the end of the day they had formed a tentative relationship because my father could see that David wasn't afraid to get his hands dirty and that he respected Dad's skill. From that time onwards, when he was in his cups Dad would implore me to 'Sign the papers, sign the papers', something I was reluctant to do, having failed the first time. When David and I did get married, we informed my parents only after the deed was done, and Dad's first reaction was to give David an extremely long handshake before asking him if he would like to go out to our former boarder Addie's farm the next day to 'pop' some tree stumps.

Like many of his generation, Dad was obsessed with the notion of make-do and mend. This often had startling results. While he was still working at the quarry at Ihumātao, he started to use scoria as a creative outlet. He cemented scoria boulders to one side of the front steps at 37 Landscape Road and installed a fish tank on a pile of scoria between the sitting and dining rooms. The fish had no complaints, but the scoria could tear stockings to shreds, as we discovered to our secret delight when the Waikato cousin came to visit.

The scoria-clad letterbox resembled a bunker, and the postman would hesitate before pushing any mail into the slot, fearful of scraping his fingers. Dad cemented lumps of scoria into the façade of the fireplace, too, but the pièce de résistance was his scoria fire screen, so heavy that only he could lift it into place at winter's end. He had cemented rocks into a frame and screwed a metal drawer handle on the top to assist with its movement; it even had a wooden ledge on which to balance a plant.

Over the years my parents had planted the stretch of grass that still resembled the field in which my maternal grandparents had kept their donkey with haphazard trees and shrubs. Long after we'd all left home, my mother met a delightful if somewhat eccentric English couple on the bus and invited them for afternoon tea in the garden. My father grumpily refused to join them until he heard them laughing and couldn't bear to be left out. They became the best of friends, Dad driving the Topps on errands every week and earning himself the nickname 'Gentleman Jack'. After he retired, he joined the Epsom Bowling Club, where it's possible he may have come into contact with former soldiers or POWs.

The delightful neighbour who lived in the rather grand house above us on the hill knew there were tensions at home. When her husband had a cerebral haemorrhage in his fifties, Dad informed her quietly that he wished it could have been him. She told me this years later, and when I said he could be difficult, she nodded, replying, 'Even so, he was a lovely man.'

And it is true that Dad became much milder as he aged. In their early seventies, he and Mum went on a tour of the South Island, visiting his old haunts in Central Otago. In Milton they met up with his mother's best friend and confidant, Mrs Milligan, and Dad took the opportunity to ask if she could confirm his parentage. With his little camera he captured the gloriously sunny weather, my mother gazing across to the Remarkables from the gondola café in Queenstown, or merely looking happily at a wandering chook.

I visited my parents soon after they returned, and Dad talked about their visit to Milton. He told me a cock and bull story about his mother conceiving him while working in a big house in Tasmania. I had long known who his real father was and was shocked that even now he couldn't face the truth, even if he was only trying to protect me. My parents had obviously had a very happy time on their holiday, and he said to me later, 'Don't tease your mother, she's my best friend.'

Once when we were driving down to visit the Waikato cousin after she had had a stroke, my mother confided in her euphemistic manner that things had been a bit difficult once but she knew Dad would never leave his children. This was the first hint I had that Mum knew what had happened during his time at Whatawhata.

And it became evident that with no parents to turn to, my mother had shared her marital difficulties with the aunt who had lent him money. When the aunt died, she left everything in equal shares to all my mother's generation except the Waikato cousin, whose name was crossed out in her will. Unable to bear the idea of a family rift, my mother persuaded the other beneficiaries to give the cousin her share. 'Well, you know, her mother died when she was just a child,' she explained. Somehow, she could always find the goodness in people.

18.

Final struggle

In 1985, my father was diagnosed with lung cancer. I took him to the hospital for surgery, and was allowed to sit with him before he was wheeled into theatre. My mother stayed at home, unable to bear the worry of it all. One lung was excised, but cancer remained centrally, where the bronchi join the trachea, impossible to remove. After two weeks, Dad was sent home, and he refused to return to the doctor despite his increasing pain.

When he started coughing up blood again, my mother covered a cardboard box with rather nasty, beige-flecked wallpaper as a receptacle for stained tissues, which she took down for burning in our old concrete incinerator in the garden, fearful of contamination. Dad must have known that his days were numbered. He added a codicil to his will, leaving his body to the university's school of medicine, or to any other similar institution in New Zealand, in the hope of saving my mother the expense of a funeral.

Two weeks before he died, I finally drove him in his much-loved Holden Kingswood to his doctor, who was appalled that Dad had struggled on without pain relief for so long. On one of my daily visits, I found a cheery nun with a fetching wimple who had come from the Mercy Hospice to check on his progress. On the day he couldn't get out of bed, the ambulance came. The drivers had some difficulty negotiating the stretcher past the scoria that lined the side of the front steps, but they eventually loaded Dad in and I followed the ambulance in his car.

The Mercy Hospice was then situated on Mountain Road, and Dad was placed in a room on the top floor with a view of Maungawhau Mount Eden, the maunga we gazed at every day from Landscape Road. After a visit from a young doctor, who asked Dad the routine questions about his date of birth and current address and examined his fingernails (I still do not know why, but perhaps they are an indicator of decline), I was left to tell Dad that there was no longer any treatment he could have.

When my son came to say goodbye, Dad struggled out of bed, determined that his grandson would think him strong to the last. My mother and younger brother arrived, but Mike was too distressed to stay long and took Mum home again. The next day Dad gradually slipped into a coma, and in the late afternoon, when the nurses suggested I take a break, I drove his car to Ponsonby to have a quick meal with friends. Just as I was about to leave, the call came, and I raced back to the hospice only to find the main door locked.

A chase worthy of an English cop show ensued as I ran frantically around the building trying to find a way in. After that I had difficulty finding the lift. Somehow it seemed a fitting finale to the chaos of our earlier lives. By the time I reached his room Dad had died, although the nurses assured me they had told him I was coming.

Perhaps he wanted to spare me the sight of him gasping for breath. He was propped upright, like a Baroque painting of the death of Saint Jerome, his face still showing signs of recent struggle. I was led into the adjoining chapel while they attended to him. When my mother and brothers arrived, he was lying flat and covered with a white sheet up to his neck, a red rose between his hands. None of us commented on how incongruous that seemed. A lump of scoria would have been more fitting.

My older brother went to Dad's side and leaned over, pressing firmly on his chest as if laying fear to rest. It was 28 January 1987, and Dad was 72 years old. His death certificate noted his cancer and recorded the immediate cause of death as 'Anorexia, exhaustion — 30 days', a statement that upset my mother as she thought it meant she hadn't fed him properly. True to form, even Dad's final wishes went awry, because on the day he died there was a surfeit of corpses at the medical school.

Down in the garden Dad had created a large barbecue area — its concreted scoria bench was lethal if you sat carelessly — adjacent to a scoria bird bath too shallow for birds to bathe in, and a rickety table with various coloured pieces of rock held in place by a frame of untreated wood. Two beer cans filled with concrete and painted the same dried-blood brown that Dad had once bought in bulk from a remainder store held up each corner.

On the day after he died, we stood in the garden, the sunshine a balm after the anguish of the previous days. One of my brothers idly nudged the table with his toe, and we collapsed with laughter as it swayed back and forth before breaking apart. Dad had forgotten to put in any reinforcing rods. Perhaps he had been harking back to his prison camp days, when tins were fashioned into a wide variety of useful or decorative items.

At his funeral we draped his coffin with the national flag, an honour allowed past service people, on top of which I placed a large, unruly

My parents on a camping holiday in Northland, early 1960s.

spray of leaves from his favourite plants from the garden. I had written the eulogy, which was delivered by a clergyman who kept veering off my text to insert references to God. We found out later that he was in the early stages of dementia. Perhaps he found my mentions of scoria inappropriate, but it seemed more accurate to us than speaking of heaven.

Later, I scattered Dad's ashes around the summit of Maungakiekie with a friend. I sensed the sacred nature of the maunga, and with Dad's volcanic nature, his love of 'the rock' and his long working life at Ihumātao, it seemed a fitting resting place.

When my mother died eight years later, it was a different story. First, a friend and I couldn't get the ugly grey plastic container that contained her ashes open, and we had to resort to using a penknife, much to the bewilderment of a busload of tourists. I had somehow imagined her ashes melding with those of my father, now long gone, but she'd obviously had quite enough of that, for she rose up and drifted off towards home, though not before a gust blew part of her back to settle all over me and I had to go to a friend's house nearby and wash her off.

Loss is a complicated experience, for it seems that parents never leave us. Twelve years after my mother died, I was working at Auckland Art Gallery Toi o Tāmaki when we moved into the Bledisloe Building for the duration of the gallery's refurbishment. Once settled in, our kaumātua Arnold Manaaki Wilson came to bless the office spaces. We followed him from cubicle to cubicle, lightly touching each of the walls. When he came to reception, he spoke softly to the newly appointed receptionist, telling her not to worry, as her parent was all right. Her face flushed and tears ran down her cheeks, for unbeknown to us her father had passed away a fortnight before. He delivered a similar message to one of our photographers.

When we returned to the other end of the floor and entered my cluttered little space, Arnold looked at me and said he would return later. Bemused, I waited. Eventually, he came back, and stood and paused a moment, before saying, 'It's very crowded — there are two other people in here.' He then described them: a larger man and a tiny woman with white hair.

It took me some time to regain my composure, but when I did I asked Arnold if the two figures were arguing. He chuckled, before replying that people couldn't live together for that long without having a few squabbles. I found this hugely comforting, but it also struck me that grief shadows you, lurking in your filing cabinets or in among your books, waiting for the right time to take you by surprise.

My son and me in 1966.

Postscript

Writing this book has made me think at length about those who, wittingly or otherwise, become involved in war. My father never reproached me for my strong anti-war stance in the 1970s and 1980s, and it is to my shame that it took me so long to consider what his own experience of war had been like. For those confronting combat, there must have been an awareness that pain and death were in store for others, even their closest comrades, if not for themselves.

For those of us who have never taken up arms, it is hard to imagine what that must have been like, for war promotes a 'licensed' brutality towards a nominated enemy, yet survivors must return to a society in which it is a crime to maim or kill. It is little wonder that many of those involved in conflict find it hard to come to terms with what they have experienced.

Prisoners of war expressed shock when they were captured; this was an eventuality that hadn't been part of the equation, and they were unprepared for it. Those captured early in the conflict faced an increasing risk of starvation and a wearying loss of hope as the years passed. Ironically, for many of those who survived life in the camps, repatriation brought an end to the close companionship with those on whom they depended for their survival. War may be brutal, but literature tells us that the comradeship and the heightened drama of battle can also make us exquisitely aware of the sweetness of life. POWs had lost their freedom, but many built close bonds with fellow prisoners — they were in it together, even if that camaraderie could be fractured at a sudden order to split up and move to different locations.

And although war trained you to suppress your own fears in the face of the enemy, it didn't train you to deal with the peace that followed. The loss of structure at war's end often gave rise to confusion and guilt as men (and women) reflected on what they had seen and had, or hadn't, done. The repercussions of this continued for many repatriated soldiers who loved or tried to love in war's aftermath. Some may have looked back to happier days before they had enlisted in the hope of finding answers there. My father's childhood may have only added to his isolation.

I asked my husband David once whether he thought Dad might have been promoted while in the army if his war had turned out differently. He replied that possibly his superiors realised he was ideally suited to the roles he had; and, as it turned out, he was captured so early in the game there wasn't much opportunity for advancement. No one would call my father a hero, but he endured. And the tragedy is that he lived out his life back home feeling that for other people it had been of no consequence.

The American war photographer Lee Miller, who suffered from alcoholism and depression, also experienced flashbacks, insomnia, anxiety, addiction and emotional disconnection from the outside world. She knew she had been damaged by the war, saying, 'I got in over my head. I could never get the stench of Dachau out of my nostrils.'[1] Yet she was too distrustful of psychiatrists to seek professional help, and she was too proud, lonely and lost to confide in family and friends.

I don't think my father ever considered there might be help available to ease his demons, and nor did many returned prisoners of war. Instead, they 'soldiered on', sometimes creating havoc in their wake. My father died in 1978, a year after the death of Lee Miller, and it was only in 1979 that psychiatrists defined the term post-traumatic stress disorder to describe the behavioural disorders experienced by those who had been exposed to the horrors of war.

Young men signed up for adventure, to see the world, to fight for King and Country, many believing they would be home by Christmas. In 1945, my father, a damaged man, returned to a society in which people had been advised not to ask questions and women were expected to make the best of any difficult situation. We recognise today how problematic this could be, for conflict plucks you out of a society, exposes you to various forms of hell and adventure, then drops you back from whence you came as if the experience of recent years were merely an intermission.

Time heals and anger dwindles over time, but no one could say my father had an easy life, and on occasions he ensured that we didn't either. Yet on his good days he wanted nothing more than to be a good and loving father to his family. If there is one thing I rue, it is that as a child I would lie in bed at night and whisper, 'Please, please, Mum, don't argue with him.' A child has no perception of what a woman in that kind of relationship has to tolerate, so this book is also an apology to her, and a recognition of how much she sacrificed to provide a home against the odds.

Notes

2. A difficult childhood

1 Finding Alan Dyer's books about his family history in Tasmania proved a godsend. And one of the joys of this project is that I have had renewed contact with Arnott cousins in New Zealand, who have provided me with extra information about the family.

2 Only Henry appears on the ship's passenger list, where he is described as being 23 years old and as having worked as a ploughman in Scotland.

3 When Bill went back to visit family in Tasmania, he wasn't allowed to cross the doorstep of his brother George's house. Such hypocrisy is unforgivable.

4 Rob Knight, 'A Sheffield Heritage: The Jones, Wilson & related families of Northern Tasmania & New Zealand', unpublished family memoir, 18.

5 I've never thought of my father as vain, but he was immensely proud of his hair and used to lean over the bath every night and massage his scalp.

6 There are very good examples in the Milton Museum.

7 Certainly, my father always gave his religion as Presbyterian, but that may have been pro forma.

8 My thanks to Keith Rogan, who gave me a copy of court records published in a local paper attesting to Mrs Milligan's unhappy home life. It reads like a script for a film: '22 November 1927, MAINTENANCE CASE. Samuel Milligan was proceeded against by his wife, Adelaide Milligan, for maintenance . . . The defendant possessed a violent temper, frequently came home drunk, smashed the crockery, and threatened to burn the house, and also to shoot plaintiff and members of the family. They had been living apart for about six years as a result. He had threatened her with a knife on several occasions. She had not asked her husband for maintenance within recent years and had not broken her husband's ribs with a hammer. The Defendant, aged 69 years, denied the greater part of his wife's allegations of cruelty, and stated that on

different occasions she had "shied" crockery at his head, smashed windows, and also chased him with a carving Knife. He had never struck his wife. He had never been drunk — "Well, not properly drunk!" On one occasion his wife "shied" a hammer and smashed three of his ribs. He possessed a good character and had never chased his family with a stockwhip. Members of the family had threatened to "bash his head in" and shoot him.' One of his sons corroborated his mother's evidence, and Mr Milligan was ordered to pay 25 shillings per week maintenance. Mr Milligan's obituary in the local paper noted that he died at the residence of his son William Milligan in 1933. 'Peace, perfect peace'. For the whole family, it would seem.

9 Carl Walrond, 'Roads — Building roads', *Te Ara — the Encyclopedia of New Zealand*, www.TeAra.govt.nz/en/roads/page-3

10 Bill and Frances stayed at Palmerston in their house on the corner of Stronsa Street until the 1950s, when they moved to Tauranga to be near Jean and her family.

11 I am extremely grateful to writer Peter Cox for alerting me to this. Cox has published two books about his own father's experiences in the Second World War (see Bibliography).

12 *Evening Star*, issue 21626, 23 January 1934, 3.

13 H. P. S., 'Topical Tattle', *Evening Star*, issue 21911, 24 December 1934, 4.

3. Life on the hill

1 Louisa turned him down when he was 13 but told him to ask again when he turned twenty-one, which he did, and she accepted.

2 Red Seal, 'Our Story', www.redseal.global/nz/our-story

4. A call to war

1 Men went to war for many reasons. Kingi Edwards, who signed up to the Māori Battalion said, 'We were tangata whenua, we belong to the land. We were fighting for what's actually ours. One of the reasons why we formed the Maori Battalion was that we wanted to go away so that we were fighting for our country. Whereas the Pakehas, they were fighting for King and Country. We went away to fight for our country. There's a bit of a difference.' Quoted in Martyn Thompson, *Our War: The grim digs — New Zealand soldiers in North Africa, 1940–1943* (Auckland: Penguin, 2005), 18–19.

2 Reported in Judith Mackrell, *Going with the Boys: Six extraordinary women writing from the Front Line* (London: Picador, 2021), 155. Shirer didn't know then that this seemingly superhuman army was thought to be fuelled by Panzerschokolade, chocolate laced with methamphetamine.

3 W. E. Murphy, *2nd New Zealand Divisional Artillery: The Third Echelon, Official History of New Zealand in the Second World War 1939–1945*

(Wellington: Historical Publications Branch, 1966), https://nzetc.victoria.ac.nz/tm/scholarly/tei-WH2Arti-c1-4.html

4 Terry Carson, 'Papakura's 1940 Influenza Epidemic', Papakura Museum Blog, papakuramuseumblog.wordpress.com/2018/02/21/papakuras-1940-influenza-epidemic

5 Auckland Teachers College in Epsom was also turned into a hospital, where my mother became an untrained nurse around 1944.

6 Carson, 'Papakura's 1940 Influenza Epidemic'.

7 The truth about Dad's parentage had never been spoken about openly in the family, and when my father wrote to Jean from Egypt to find out if what Jack York had said was true, she asked her mother, who reluctantly confirmed it.

8 S. P. Llewellyn, *Troopships* (Wellington: War History Branch, Department of Internal Affairs, 1949), 5.

9 Murphy, *Official History*, 14.

10 Ibid., 15.

5. Egypt

1 Terry Vaughan, *Whistle as You Go: The story of the Kiwi concert party and Terry Vaughan* (Auckland: Random House, 1995), 17.

2 Quoted in Megan Hutching (ed.) with Ian McGibbon, *The Desert Road: New Zealanders remember the North African campaign* (Auckland: HarperCollins, 2005), 9.

3 Anthony Madden, *Egypt, 'Land of the Pharaohs'*, unpublished memoir, 8, quoted in Alex Hedley with Megan Hutching, *Fernleaf Cairo: New Zealanders at Maadi Camp* (Auckland: HarperCollins, 2009), 23.

4 Captain Peter McIntyre, 'An Artist's Trials', Address to the Otago Art Society, 1943, reported in *Dunedin Evening Star*, 10 August 1943, quoted in Jennifer Haworth, *The Art of War: New Zealand war artists in the Field 1939–1945. Peter McIntyre, Austen Deans, Allan Barns-Graham, Russell Clark, John McIndoe* (Christchurch: Hazard Press, 2007), 89.

5 Anonymous diary, October 1943, 'From Cairo to Italy, 2006, 1339 (Kippenberger Military Archive), quoted in Hedley and Hutching, *Fernleaf Cairo*, 121.

6 Robin Kay, *27 (Machine Gun) Battalion* (Wellington: Historical Publishing Branch, Department of Internal Affairs, 1958), 14.

7 Donald Haddon, quoted in Martyn Uren, *Kiwi Saga: Memoirs of a New Zealand artilleryman* (Auckland: Collins, 1946), 177–78.

8 Quoted by Lieutenant-General The Rt Hon Sir Jerry Mateparae, GNZM, QSO in a speech given to his alma mater, Wellington College, Thursday, 1 August 2013, https://gg.govt.nz/publications/freyberg-lecture

9 Interview between Tony Martin and Peter McIntyre, 18 August 1979, quoted in Haworth, *The Art of War*, 113.

10 Hedley and Hutching, *Fernleaf Cairo*, 30–31.

11 The verso of photographs, like those of paintings, can be very revealing. The stamp on the back indicates that the photography paper was Velox, a type invented in the late nineteenth century. The printed stamp of 152 suggests that this may have been an official photograph rather than an amateur one.
12 Hedley and Hutching, *Fernleaf Cairo*, 30–31.
13 Australian War Memorial, 'Cairo, Egypt. 1941–08. A group portrait taken at the Heliopolis racecourse of members of HQ AIF, Middle East', www.awm.gov.au/collection/C297967
14 I still have a small notebook that records the horses Dad bet on, and how much he won or lost over the years.
15 Hedley and Hutching, *Fernleaf Cairo*, 117.

6. To Greece and back again

1 George Kaye and Peter Bates, 'Baptism of Fire: 40th Anniversary of the campaigns in Greece and Crete' (Lower Hutt: INL Print Ltd, n.d.), E. H. (Ted) Everton POW Papers, folder 1, MS 2000/21, Auckland War Memorial Museum Library.
2 Martyn Thompson, *Our War: The grim digs — New Zealand soldiers in North Africa, 1940–1943* (Auckland: Penguin, 2005), 53.
3 Extracts from Interview with Sir Charles Bennett, interviewer Jim Sullivan, recorded 31 March and 1 April 1993, commissioned by the Ministry of External Relations, https://www.28maoribattalion.org.nz/audio/charles-bennett-describes-freezing-conditions-mt-olympus-greece.
4 W. G. McClymont, *To Greece* (Wellington: Historical Publications Branch, 1959), 138, quoted in W. E. Murphy, *2nd New Zealand Divisional Artillery: The Third Echelon, Official History of New Zealand in the Second World War 1939–1945* (Wellington: Historical Publications Branch, 1966), 26.
5 Thompson, *Our War*, 55.
6 Jack certainly passed through Katerini, but he never named the village where the accident had taken place.
7 Murphy, *Official History*, 54.
8 New Zealand War Graves Project, 'Norman Alexander Mackay', www.nzwargraves.org.nz/casualties/norman-alexander-mackay
9 Captain Charles Upham, letter written 7 October 1945, quoted in Noel 'Wig' Gardiner, *Freyberg's Circus: Reminiscences of a Kiwi soldier in the North African campaign of World War II* (Auckland, Sydney, London: Ray Richards/William Collins, 1981), Appendix B, 180–82.
10 S. P. Llewellyn, *Journey towards Christmas: Official History of the 1st Ammunition Company Second New Zealand Expeditionary Force, 1939–45* (Wellington: War History Branch, Department of Internal Affairs, 1949), 122.
11 McClymont, *To Greece*, 356.
12 Murphy, *Official History*, 590–92.
13 Thompson, *Our War*, 60.

14 'The Battle of Crete', Auckland War Memorial Museum Tāmaki Paenga Hira, https://www.aucklandmuseum.com/discover/collections/topics/the-battle-of-crete
15 Interview with Watt McEwan, 16 May 2003, Watt McEwan and Watt Nelson, 1919–2015, National Library, Wellington, OHInt-0798-10. https://natlib.govt.nz/records/35853232
16 'Report by Major-General B. C. Freyberg on the Operations of the 2nd New Zealand Division in Greece and Crete, delivered to the Minister of Defence, and presented to both Houses of the General Assembly on 9 Oct 1941', http://nzetc.victoria.ac.nz/tm/scholarly/tei-WH2-2Doc-c2.html
17 The American Presidency Project, 'A Letter Praising the Heroism of the Greeks', www.presidency.ucsb.edu/documents/letter-praising-the-heroism-the-greeks
18 Illustrated History: Relive the Times, https://incredibleimages4u.blogspot.com/2011/04/german-invades-greece-crete-1941.html
19 www.ww2wrecks.com/portfolio/the-nazi-occupation-of-greece-1941-44-an-endless-list-of-crimes-atrocities-and-bloodbaths/
20 https://www.aucklandmuseum.com/discover/collections/topics the-battle-of-crete

7. The Battle of Sidi Rezegh

1 Donald McDonald, *Sidi Rezegh and Other Verses,* (Wellington: Progressive Publishing Society for Feilding Agriculture High School Old Pupils Association, 1944), 11, quoted in John Crawford (ed.), *Kia Kaha: New Zealand in the Second World War* (Auckland: Oxford University Press, 2000), 1.
2 Geoffrey Cox, *A Tale of Two Battles: A personal memoir of Crete and the Western Desert 1941* (London: William Kimber, 1987), 150.
3 Stephen Kirrage, Egypt & Cyrenaica, Libya: Map of the Western Desert Campaign and its Operation Compass Battle Area 1941, 14 October 2007, https://commons.wikimedia.org/wiki/File:WesternDesertBattle_Area1941_en.svg
4 'Far History S. Africa Views the Sidi Rezegh Battles', *Press* (Christchurch), issue 28553, 5 April 1958, 3.
5 Cox, *A Tale of Two Battles*, 148–151.
6 Ibid., 139.
7 Ibid., 134.
8 H. K. Kippenberger, *Infantry Brigadier: The author's experiences in Greece, North Africa and Italy from 1939 to 1944* (London: Cumberledge, 1949), 94–95.
9 There proved to be a connection between the two, for at the end of fighting in Tunisia in May the following year, the defeated Africa Division demanded the right to surrender to the Kiwis.
10 Quoted in 'Germans Offer Desperate Resistance', London, 28 November 1941, received 28 November, 11 p.m.; reprinted in *Press*, 29 November 1941, 9.
11 '"A Tremendous 24 Hours", Battles in Desert on Tuesday — Both sides lose heavily', received November 28, 12.55, *Press*, issue 23498, 28 November 1941, 7.

12 Accounts in regard to night action can confuse. They are generally given the date of the day the action commenced, even though prolonged fighting may have continued well into the next day.
13 Held in the private collection of the Hon. Sir John White, published in Matthew Wright, *Freyberg: A life's journey* (Auckland: Oratia Books, 2020).
14 Cox, *A Tale of Two Battles*, 199.

8. Capture

1 Although the shrapnel has been lost, I have recently gifted my father's hei-tiki to my son in Australia.
2 W. Wynne Mason, *Prisoners of War, Official History of New Zealand in the Second World War, 1939–45* (Wellington: War History Branch, Department of Internal Affairs, 1954), 104–5.
3 Arthur Drower, 'The Bardia Diary 1941–1942', Auckland Museum Library, MS 2002/46.
4 Jim Henderson, quoted in Thompson, *Our War*, 243.
5 Major Harry Sell, in Peter Liddle and Ian Whitehead, 'Not the Image but Reality: British POW experiences in Italian and German camps', https://war-experience.org/events/british-pow-experiences-in-italian-and-german-camps/
6 Will Rapson, quoted in Thompson, *Our War*, 244–45.
7 Tom Straker, quoted in ibid., 242.
8 The Red Cross was set up in 1859 by Swiss national Henry Dunant, to aid soldiers of all nations who were injured or taken prisoner during wartime, working closely with the Order of Saint John.
9 I did not know that as early as 1941 the public was well aware of the difference between camps that held POWs and those that held people according to their religious, genetic, political or social status.
10 If the flight was via Lisbon, the letter or card cost 3 shillings; by air to New York, thence by surface mail to Lisbon 2 shillings; by surface mail to USA, thence by air to Lisbon 1 shilling. There were also flights to Cape Town, thence by surface mail to London (where all the mail was sorted before being forwarded to the camps), using the Empire Air Service. Examples of these forms are included in the archive of Captain F. W. O. Jones, Auckland War Memorial Museum, Frederick William Osborn Jones — Second World War letters, 1940–1946, MS-2007-47; 2007/47; Folder 3.

9. The journey to Campo PG 66, Capua

1 Quoted in Adrian Gilbert, *POW Allied Prisoners in Europe 1939 to 1945* (London: John Murray, 2006), 51.
2 Allies in Italy, 'PG 66 Capua', www.alleatiinitalia.it/en/camps/camp-tab/?ricerca=15

3 I have no personal records of my father's time at PG 66, apart from the bare facts listed in his Army Record and therefore have had to rely on information supplied by other POWs, archival material and invaluable websites.
4 Allies in Italy. Both *Campifascitisti.it* and *alleatiinitalia.it* have been invaluable sources for information about the prison camps throughout much of Italy.
5 The National Archives UK [TNA, WO 311/320], quoted in Allies in Italy, 'PG 66 Capua'.
6 International Committee of the Red Cross Audiovisual Archives, https://avarchives.icrc.or
7 Philip Green, 'Two Italian POW Camps — Capua and Monturano', WW2 — People's War BBC History Article ID: A5248334, www.bbc.co.uk/history/ww2peopleswar/stories/34/a5248334.shtml
8 Allies in Italy, 'Camp Overview', https://www.alleatiinitalia.it/en/camps/camp-tab/?ricerca=15
9 Allies in Italy.
10 There is plenty of evidence that this rule wasn't applied by the Germans as the war progressed. The Germans would frequently refuse to recognise ranks as being of NCO status even after the British Government had sent proof of individuals' rights in this respect. This coupled with the fact that a few POW privates would pretend to have a higher rank to escape compulsory work meant that anyone below a significant rank would struggle in choosing not to work. The Wartimes Memories Project, https://wartimememoriesproject.com/ww2/pow/powcamp.php?pid=3320
11 Dan Billany and David Dowie, *The Cage* (London: Longmans, 1945),12 e, 25–26.
12 Dan Billany in Midge Gillies, The *Barbed-Wire University: The real lives of Allied prisoners of war in the Second World War* (London: Aurum Press, 2012), 51.
13 The Order of Saint John also supported POWs with food parcels and essential items.
14 New Zealanders also sent care packages to England during rationing. My husband David remembers receiving one in England as a child, but something sticky had leaked over all the contents, making them unusable.
15 Allies in Italy, TNA, WO 311/331.
16 Allies in Italy.
17 WW2Talk, 'Capua, PG 66', ww2talk.com/index.php?threads/capua-pg-66.69202

10. PG 52, Chiavari, Pian di Coreglia

1 Giorgio 'Getto' Viarengo, *Documenti per una storia del fascismo nel circondario di Chiavari* (*The history of Fascism in Chiavari as recorded in contemporary documents*), reproduced in a book and on a website about the Caserma di Caperana — the Signals Academy at Caperana, Chiavari, https://powcamp52.weebly.com/

2 Ibid.

3 Recorded in W. Wynne Mason, *Prisoners of War, Official History of New Zealand in the Second World War, 1939–45* (Wellington: War History Branch, Department of Internal Affairs, 1954), 119.

4 Ibid., 120.

5 These moved from very primitive to sophisticated devices as the war progressed. For a lively outline of their use, see New Zealand History Online, https://nzhistory.govt.nz/war/second-world-war/prisoners-of-war/camp-cookers

6 The 14 lunettes still extant are now permanently displayed at Villa Petraia, outside of Florence.

7 Jock Fraser's drawings and paintings are now held at Aigantighe Art Gallery, Timaru, which produced a beautiful book of his collection in 2023 to accompany the exhibition *Jock Fraser — Artist in the Tempest,* (23 November 2023–12 February 2024). I am deeply grateful to Aigantighe Art Gallery Manager Cara Fitzgerald for sending me a copy of the catalogue.

8 Tom Lubbock, 'Dürer, Albrecht: The Large Turf (1503)', *Independent*, 18 January 2008.

9 Fraser was later transferred to Campo 57 at the end of 1942, four months before Jack.

10 Extract from the British *Prisoners of War Relatives Association*, news sheet October 1942, reproduced in the *New Zealand POWRA*, no. 14, April 1943.

11 Tim Healey, *Come on Lads: Canteen songs of the Second World War performed by Sods' Opera* (Royal British Legion and Beautiful Jo Records, 1965) contains a selection of these ballads, many of which are vulgar but very funny rewrites of familiar tunes, such as 'My bomber lies over the ocean', and 'I haven't seen old Hitler'.

12 Malcolm J. Mason, *The Water Flows Uphill: A Kiwi Returns to Italy* (London: Allen & Unwin; Auckland: Blackwood & Janet Paul, 1964), 71.

13 Megan Hutching and Ian McGibbon (eds), *Inside Stories: New Zealand POWs remember the Second World War* (Auckland: HarperCollins, 2005), 208.

14 Ibid., 207.

15 Midge Gillies, *The Barbed-Wire University: The real lives of Allied prisoners of war in the Second World War* (London: Aurum Press, 2012), 21.

16 W. A. Weakley, 'Camp 52, for prisoners of war, Chiavari, Italy, 1942', Department of Internal Affairs, War History Branch, World War 1939–1945 official negatives — DA Series: Ref. DA-00376. https://natlib.govt.nz/records/22876238

17 'POW Kodak camera', New Zealand History Online (Ministry for Culture and Heritage), https://nzhistory.govt.nz/media/photo/kodak-camera

18 'Prisoners of war held in Campo PG 52 Pian di Coreglia (Chiavari), March 1942–March 1943', https://powcamp52.weebly.com/uploads/6/6/7/2/6672243/pg-52-nos-prisoners_1_orig.jpg

11. PG 57, Gruppignano

1 Basil Borthwick, 'Campo 57, Italy, September 1943 What Really Happened', *New Zealand POW Magazine*, n.p.

2 Campo 57 Grupignano/San Mauro, http://campo57.com/

3 D. O. W. Hall, 'Prisoners of Italy — Gruppignano', *The Official History of New Zealand in the Second World War, Episodes & Studies Vol. 1*, 77–78, https://nzetc.victoria.ac.nz/tm/scholarly/tei-WH2-1Epi-c4-WH2-1Epi-i.html

4 Malcolm J. Mason, The Water Flows Uphill: A Kiwi returns to Italy (London: Allen & Unwin; Auckland: Blackwood & Janet Paul, 1964), 216.

5 The road leading to the chapel also has a deep canal on the far side, which was empty when I visited in early autumn.

6 Hall, 'Prisoners of Italy', 6–7.

7 Quoted in Australian War Memorial, 'Stolen Years', https://www.awm.gov.au/visit/exhibitions/stolenyears/ww2/italy/story2

8 Ibid.

9 Adrian Gilbert, *POW Allied Prisoners in Europe 1939 to 1945* (London: John Murray, 2006), 74.

10 Hall, 'Prisoners of Italy', 77.

11 Gilbert, *POW Allied Prisoners in Europe 1939 to 1945*, 169.

12 Mason, *The Water Flows Uphill*, 47.

13 Herbert Jack Wesley, 1916–2007, Megan Hutching interviews, Alexander Turnbull Library Tape numbers — OHC-011737–OHC-011739, Ref: OHInt-0802-09, later published in Megan Hutching and Ian McGibbon (eds), *Inside Stories: New Zealand POWs remember the Second World War* (Auckland: HarperCollins, 2005), 134–35.

14 Paul Grey and Sally Grey, 'Private J. D. Caves: The Long Journey Home', New Zealand Texts Collection, 85. https://nzetc.victoria.ac.nz/tm/scholarly/tei-GreLong-t1-body-d7-d14.html

15 Grupignano — Campo per prigionieri di guerra n. 57, PGGU03, PGGU04, PGGU05 and PGGU06. https://campifascisti.it/scheda_campo.php?id_campo=353

16 Grupignano — Campo per prigionieri di guerra n. 57, PGCH01 and PGGU01.

17 Steve Liddell, *The War Inside: New Zealand prisoners of war tell their stories* (Feilding: Brebner Print, 2023), 120.

18 There is a Stephen Oliver (24951) listed in Stalag XVIII-A, Wolfsberg, Austria, who may well have been in Gruppignano, but there are no other details on the Online Cenotaph. Nor have I traced some of the other names Dad mentioned.

19 Hall, 'Prisoners of Italy — Gruppignano', 7.

20 Paula Legel, Associate Curator, Heritage Publications at Auckland War Memorial Museum, was travelling with me as we had another research project we were working on as well. She was immensely supportive in relation to my father, having carried out similar research into her own father's experiences

in Burma, understanding the sharp wave of emotion when a piece of personal history is revealed for the first time.

21 Unlike many former POW camps, Gruppignano is easy to locate by searching 'Chiesetta PG 57' on Google Earth.

22 Campo 57 Grupignano/San Mauro.

23 Jennifer Mallison, *From Taranto to Trieste: Following the 2nd Division's Italian campaign, 1943–45* (Masterton: Fraser Books, 2019), 272.

12. PG 103/6, Ampezzo

1 James McNeill Whistler famously painted his mother seated in profile, in widow's weeds, wearing a little white cap.

2 Albergo Diffuso Sauris, 'The dam and the lake of Lumiei'. www.albergodiffusosauris.com/en/the-dam-and-the-lake-of-lumiei/

3 Megan Hutching and Ian McGibbon (eds), *Inside Stories: New Zealand POWs remember the Second World War* (Auckland: HarperCollins, 2005), 210

4 Prisoners of War: Online memorial and museum, 'German Seizure of British POWs from the Italians.' www.prisonersofwarmuseum.com/german-seizure-of-british-pows-from-the-italians

5 The loss of teeth caused unending discomfort for many POWs, especially when they were forced to survive hard tack, which could only be chewed if you had strong teeth or if it was soaked in water. Men were often forced to break it up with their fingers and 'mumble' it soft before swallowing.

6 Albergo Diffuso Sauris.

13. Stalag XI-A, Altengrabow

1 Megan Hutching and Ian McGibbon (eds), *Inside Stories: New Zealand POWs remember the Second World War* (Auckland: HarperCollins, 2005), 211.

2 I have never visited the sites of the two main camps where my father was listed in Germany. Although listed at Stalags XI-A and XI-B, Jack was also in unidentified work camps, and nothing amongst his memorabilia gave me any clues. I have learned enough from films, books, and so on, and though it may seem cowardly, I don't wish to be confronted with what happened in Nazi Germany first hand. All the photographs of Dad in Italy show a man who is coping and who can still smile, whereas in Germany the hardships experienced by prisoners and ordinary people alike robbed him of something, as evidenced in the photograph taken when he was finally liberated.

3 'Germany and German Occupied Territories Imperial Prisoners of War Alphabetical List: Section 4: New Zealand: 2nd New Zealand Expeditionary Force', *Zenodo*, https://zenodo.org/record/3632116

4 'Stalag XI-A Altengrabow', *Sergeant Detmar*, http://sergeantdetmar.nl/stalag-xi-a-alten-grabow

5 John McIndoe's mother, Mabel Hill, was also an artist, while his brother Archibald McIndoe was the famous plastic surgeon who revolutionised the treatment of badly burned and disfigured airmen during the Second World War.
6 Adrian Gilbert, *POW Allied Prisoners in Europe 1939 to 1945* (London: John Murray, 2006), 124.
7 Ibid., 271.
8 Ibid., 131.
9 A. T. Casdagli, *Prouder than Ever: My war, my diary, my embroidery* (London: Cylix Press, 2014), 66.
10 Ibid., 76.

14. Stalag XI-B, Fallingbostel

1 In March 1945, a month before liberation, all the NCOs were forced to leave once more.
2 Jennifer Haworth, *The Art of War: New Zealand war artists in the Field 1939–1945. Peter McIntyre, Austen Deans, Allan Barns-Graham, Russell Clark, John McIndoe* (Christchurch: Hazard Press, 2007), 83.
3 Ken Fenton, 'Ken Fenton's War', https://kenfentonswar.com/stalag-357
4 Ted Everton, letter written 4 November 1944, published in The New Zealand *Prisoners of War* Pamphlet, 29 March 1945, 8.
5 Fenton, 'Ken Fenton's War', 5.
6 https://en.wikipedia.org/wiki/Bombing_of_Braunschweig_(October_1944).
7 Richard Campbell Begg and Peter Little, *For Five Shillings a Day: Anzacs and Allies Fighting in the Second World War* (London: HarperCollins, 2000), 334.
8 Major Harry Sell, in Peter Liddle and Ian Whitehead, 'Not the Image but Reality: British POW experiences in Italian and German camps'. https://war-experience.org/events/british-pow-experiences-in-italian-and-german-camps
9 Steve Liddle, *The War Inside: New Zealand Prisoners of War Tell Their Stories* (Feilding: Brebner Print, 2023). While the Online Cenotaph at Auckland War Memorial Museum lists a J. Barber, with no further information, in the list of 2NZEF prisoners held in Germany there is a Private J. R. Barber, whose New Zealand number was 23443, and his German POW number 6522. Whether that is the individual Liddle is referring to is unknown.
10 Daniel Jonah Goldhagen, *Hitler's Willing Executioners: Ordinary Germans and the Holocaust* (London and Auckland: Little, Brown/ Random House, 1996), 268–69.
11 Interview in *Otago Daily Times*, issue 25914, 4 August 1945, 4.
12 Gilbert, *Allied Prisoners*, 231.
13 Watkins had also been imprisoned at Gruppignano, but moved to Stalag IV-G, Oschatz, in Saxony.
14 Charles James Watkins: Research papers relating to prisoner of war (Miscellaneous papers relating to prisoners of war), Alexander Turnbull Library, MS-Papers-8627-09, 30.

15 Fenton, 'Ken Fenton's War', 24.
16 'Ken Brown and the Stalag XIB (357) Memorial, 207 Squadron Royal Air Force History, http://www.207squadron.rafinfo.org.uk/stalag_XIB_ken_brown.htm
17 David McGill, with Radio NZ Sound Archives, *P.O.W.: The untold stories of New Zealanders as prisonerss of war* (Naenae: Mills Publications, 1987), 138–39.
18 Victor E. Frankl, *Man's Search for Meaning* (London, Sydney, Auckland, Johannesburg: Rider, 2004), 37.
19 Judith Mackrell, *Going with the Boys: Six extraordinary women writing from the Front Line* (London: Picador, 2021), 316.
20 Megan Hutching and Ian McGibbon (eds), *Inside Stories: New Zealand POWs remember the Second World War* (Auckland: HarperCollins, 2005), 213.
21 '"Richard Dimbleby Describes Belsen", BBC News, April 15, 1945', BBC News, 15 April 2005, www.bbc.com/videos/c87z7poj3g5o

15. Repatriation

1 W. Wynne Mason, *Prisoners of War, Official History of New Zealand in the Second World War, 1939–45* (Wellington: War History Branch, Department of Internal Affairs, 1954), 119. Author's asterisk.
2 'Repatriated Men', Waikato Times, 28 March 1945, 2. https://paperspast.natlib.govt.nz/newspapers/WT19450328.2.3
3 W. Wynne Mason, 'Prisoners in the United Kingdom and their Repatriation' in Mason, *Prisoners of War*.
4 When the camps were opened, some prisoners died from eating more than their digestive systems could cope with.
5 'Repatriated Men', *Waikato Times*, issue 22572, 28 March 1945, 2.
6 Wilfred Owen, Letter to his mother dated 28 December 1916, https://britainsbestguides.org/blogs/folkestone-a-quiet-seaside-resort-at-war
7 Leslie Jones, 'The History of the Hotel Metropole (1897) and the New Metropole (1961) in Folkestone', *Cantium* (Autumn 1974), n.p.
8 Keppell was the great-great-grandmother of Queen Camilla of England.
9 Unpublished document held at the Folkestone Library and Archive. Poorly funded, the archive holds several boxes of ephemera that have not yet been catalogued. Luckily, it has a very helpful librarian.
10 Rhys Griffiths, 'The Sad Story Behind The Grand in Folkestone, One of Kent's Most Famous Hotels', *Kent Online*, 8 May 2023.
11 *Folkestone Hythe and District Herald*, 27 September 1959, 14.
12 Jones, 'History of the Hotel Metropole'.
13 Mason, *Prisoners of War*, 494.
14 Lieutenant-Colonel. A. T. M. Wilson, RAMC: Report to the War Office on the psychological aspects of the rehabilitation of repatriated prisoners of war. Quoted in Mason, *Prisoners of War*.
15 Midge Gillies, *The Barbed-Wire University: The real lives of Allied prisoners of war in the Second World War* (London: Aurum Press, 2012), 426.

16 Ted Everton, quoted in 'Odd Getting Used to Freedom', *New Zealand Free Lance*, newspaper cutting, MS 2000/21, Everton, E. H. (Ted), POW Papers, Auckland War Memorial Museum.
17 Tony Vercoe, *Yesterday's Drums: Echoes from the Wasteland of War* (Wellington: Steele Roberts, 2001), 193, quoted in Mathew Johnson, 'Identity and Remembrance in the New Zealand Ex-Prisoners of War Association after the Second World War', *Journal of Veterans Studies*, Vol. 6, 1 (2020), 36–45, https: /doi.org/10.21061/jvs.v6i1.154
18 Jack Rae, *Kiwi Spitfire Ace: A Gripping World War II Story of Action, Captivity, and Freedom* (London: Grub Street, 2001), 168–69, quoted in Johnson, 'Identity and Remembrance', 37.

16. The return home

1 'Italy, 28 February 1945 BC Freyberg, Lt-General, Commanding 2nd NZ Division, and 2nd NZEF', reproduced in Martyn Uren, *Diamond Trails of Italy* (Auckland: Collins, 1945), postscript.
2 David McGill, with Radio NZ Sound Archives, *P.O.W.: The untold stories of New Zealanders as prisoners of war* (Naenae: Mills Publications, 1987), 156.
3 Malcolm J. Mason, *The Water Flows Uphill: A Kiwi returns to Italy* (London: Allen & Unwin; Auckland: Blackwood & Janet Paul, 1964), viii..
4 Christopher Pugsley, *A Bloody Road Home: World War Two and New Zealand's heroic Second Division* (Auckland: Penguin, 2014), 242, quoted in Johnson, 'Identity and Remembrance in the New Zealand Ex-Prisoners of War Association after the Second World War', 36–45.
5 J. Hagger, questionnaire, 30 August 1999, quoted in Martin Crotty and Marina Larsson (eds), *ANZAC Legacies: Australians and the Aftermath of War* (Melbourne: Australian Scholarly Publishing, 2010), 112.
6 J. Gallichan (ed.), *The Tiki Times: A Souvenir Booklet of the Camp Newspaper for Prisoners-of-war* (Palmerston North: Keeling & Mundy Ltd, 1950), 1.
7 *POW WOW*, June 1989, 5.

17. Aftermath

1 Notes by Winifred Ramsay (née Gray), circa 1988, transcribed by her son Graham Ramsay for a family memoir, April 2011.
2 *Otago Daily Times*, issue 25914, 4 August 1945, 4.
3 Mary Pethybridge had married my great uncle Arthur immediately after First World War in Devon, before coming out to New Zealand. Arthur had been captured by the Germans at Messines after being hit by a bomb which permanently damaged his right arm. In his unpublished memoir, he records the humour used by prisoners to defy their German captors. The men were constantly ordered to fill out forms that included their civilian occupations. One listed his as 'hot cross bun maker', while others described themselves as

inspectors of fire escapes, dolls'-eye makers, theatre-door operators, and, from a Scotsman, a coronation-programme seller. The best, however, according to Uncle Arthur, was the Australian who claimed to work as a boundary-rider on a bee farm.

4 Football was a favourite sport in our household, and my brothers were also prone to kicking the ball over the back hedge, damaging the glasshouse in the Whineray garden, infuriating Mrs Whineray but possibly amusing her famous footballer son.

5 I say relative, because when he blew up the rocks for the foundations of the 246 development in Queen Street, the explosion accidently broke all the windows in Woolworths next door.

Postscript

1 Quoted in 'Troubled Witness', *Economist*, 1 December 2005, www.economist.com/books-and-arts/2005/12/01/troubled-witness

Bibliography

Begg, Richard Campbell and Peter Liddell, *For Five Shillings a Day: ANZACS and Allies fighting in the Second World War* (London: HarperCollins, 2000).

Casdagli, A. T., compiled by Alexis Penny Casdagli, *Prouder than Ever: My war, my diary, my embroidery* (London: Cylix Press, 2014).

Collinson, Roger, '"March 1943". Diaries written by Roger Collinson whilst a prisoner of World War II, 21st February 1943 to 18th May 1945', 2009.

Cox, Geoffrey, *A Tale of Two Battles: A personal memoir of Crete and the Western Desert 1941* (London: William Kimber, 1987).

Cox, Peter, *Good Luck to All the Lads: The wartime story of Brian Cox 1939–43* (Christchurch: J. J. Angerstein & Associates, 2008).

———*Desert War: The Battle of Sidi Rezegh* (Australia: Exisle Publishing, 2015).

Crawford, John (ed.), *Kia Kaha: New Zealand in the Second World War* (Auckland: Oxford University Press, 2000).

Crotty, Martin and Marina Larsson (eds), *ANZAC Legacies: Australians and the aftermath of war* (Melbourne: Australian Scholarly Publishing, 2010).

Gardiner, Noel 'Wig', *Freyberg's Circus: Reminiscences of a Kiwi soldier in the North African campaign of World War II* (Auckland, Sydney, London: Ray Richards/William Collins, 1981).

Gerard, J. D., *Unwilling Guests* (Wellington: A. H. & A. W. Reed, 1945).

Germany & German Occupied Territories: Imperial POW alphabetical and List Section 4, New_Zealand_2NZEF Version 2.csv, https://zenodo.org/record/3955186

Gilbert, Adrian, *POW: Allied prisoners in Europe 1939–1945* (London: John Murray, 2006).

Gillies, Midge, *The Barbed-Wire University: The real lives of Allied prisoners of war in the Second World War* (London: Aurum Press, 2012).

Goldhagen, Daniel Jonah, *Hitler's Willing Executioners: Ordinary Germans and the Holocaust* (London and Auckland: Little, Brown/Random House, 1996).

Hall, D. O. W., 'Prisoners of Italy', in *Episodes & Studies* Vol. 1, *Official History of New Zealand in the Second World War 1939–45* (Wellington: Historical Publications Branch, 1954).

Hargest, Brigadier James, *Farewell Campo 12* (London and Wellington: Michael Joseph/Whitcombe & Tombs, 1946).

Haworth, Jennifer, *The Art of War: New Zealand War Artists in the Field 1939–1945. Peter McIntyre, Austen Deans, Allan Barns-Graham, Russell Clark, John McIndoe* (Christchurch: Hazard Press, 2007).

Hedley, Alex with Megan Hutching, *Fernleaf Cairo: New Zealanders at Maadi Camp* (Auckland: HarperCollins, 2009).

Henderson, Jim, *Gunner Inglorious* (Wellington: Whitcombe & Tombs, 1945).

Horner, Gordon, 'For you the war is over, 1942–[ca]1950', including letters of Gray, George Duncan Dunbar, 1906–1977; Horner, Gordon, active 1939–1948; privately published (London: Falcon Press).

Hutching, Megan (ed.) with Ian McGibbon, *Inside Stories: New Zealand POWs remember the Second World War* (Auckland: HarperCollins, 2002).

———*The Desert Road: New Zealanders Remember the North African campaign* (Auckland: HarperCollins, 2005).

Jeffs, Ruth, *Jock Fraser — Artist in the Tempest* (Tīmaru: Aigantighe Art Gallery, 2023).

Johnson, M., 'Identity and Remembrance in the New Zealand Ex-Prisoners of War Association after the Second World War', *Journal of Veterans Studies*, Vol. 6: 1 (2020). http://doi.org/10.21061/jvs.v6i1.154

Jones, Leslie, 'The History of The Hotel Metropole (1897) and the New Metropole (1961) in Folkestone', *Cantium* (Autumn, 1974).

Kay, Elizabeth, *Eddie Norman and 25 Battalion* (Wellington, Cuba Press, 2019).

King, Josh, '"Certainly Getting About the World": New Zealanders' Experience of the Middle East as a Place During the Second World War', *Journal of New Zealand Studies*, NS30 (2020), https://doi.org/10.26686/jnzs.v0iNS30.6501

Lamb, Richard, *War in Italy: 1943–1945* (New York: St Martin's Press, 1994).

Liddle, Steve, *The War Inside: New Zealand Prisoners of War Tell Their Stories* (Feilding: Brebner Print, 2023).

Llewellyn, S. P., *Journey Towards Christmas: Official History of the 1st Ammunition Company Second New Zealand Expeditionary Force, 1939–45* (Wellington: War History Branch, Department of Internal Affairs, 1949).

———Llewellyn, S P., *Troopships* (Wellington: War History Branch, Department of Internal Affairs, 1949).

Mackrell, Judith, *Going with the Boys: Six extraordinary women writing from the Front Line* (London: Picador, 2021).

Mallison, Jennifer, *From Taranto to Trieste: Following the 2nd Division's Italian campaign, 1943–45* (Masterton: Fraser Books, 2019).

Mason, Malcolm J., *The Water Flows Uphill: A Kiwi Returns to Italy* (London and New Zealand: George Allen & Unwin/ Blackwood and Janet Paul, 1964).

Mason, W. Wynne, *Prisoners of War, Official History of New Zealand in the Second World War, 1939-45* (Wellington: War History Branch, Department of Internal Affairs, 1954), https://nzetc.victoria.ac.nz/tm/scholarly/tei-WH2Pris-_N78986.html

McClymont, W. G., *To Greece: Official history of New Zealand in the Second World War 1939–45* (Wellington: Historical Publications Branch, Department of Internal Affairs, 1959).

McCormick, E. H. and W. E. Glue (eds), *Campaign in Greece: The New Zealand Division in action* (Wellington: Army Board, 1943).

McGill, David, with Radio NZ Sound Archives, *P.O.W.: The untold stories of New Zealanders as prisoners of war* (Naenae: Mills Publications, 1987).

McNeish, James, *Dance of the Peacocks: New Zealanders in exile in the time of Hitler and Mao Tse-Tung* (Auckland: Vintage/Random House, 2003).

Munro, R. D., *7th N.Z. Anti-Tank Regiment, 2 NZEF, 1939–45* (Upper Hutt: R. D. Munro, 1990).

Murphy, W. E., *2nd New Zealand Divisional Artillery: Official history of New Zealand in the Second World War 1939–45* (Wellington: Historical Publications Branch, 1966).

———'Point 175: The Battle of Sunday of the Dead', in *Episodes & Studies* Vol. 2, *Official history of New Zealand in the Second World War 1939–1945* (Wellington: Historical Publications Branch, 1954), https://nzetc.victoria.ac.nz/tm/scholarly/tei-WH2-2Epi-f2-WH2-2Epi-k.html

Noice, Pearl and Ron (eds), *History of the New Zealand Ex-Prisoners of War Association (Inc.) 1946–2002* (Cambridge: New Zealand Ex-Prisoners of War Association, 2002).

Penrose, Antony (ed.), *Lee Miller's War: Photographer and Correspondent with the Allies in Europe 1944–45* (London: Condé Nast Books, 1992).

Pugsley, Christopher, *A Bloody Road Home: World War Two and New Zealand's heroic Second Division* (Auckland: Penguin, 2014).

Ranfurly, Countess of, *To War with Whitaker: The Wartime Diaries of the Countess of Ranfurly 1939–1945* (Leicester: Charnwood, 1997).

Scobie, Richard A., *Egypt* (Printing and Stationery Services, M.E.F. [1945])

Scott, Archibald, *Dark of the Moon* (New Zealand: Cresset Books, 1985).

Starace, Carlo, *A Prison Camp Diary 23 September 1943–24 September 1944* (Tīmaru: Paola Starace, 1999).

Thompson, Martyn, *Our War: The grim digs — New Zealand soldiers in North Africa, 1940–1943* (Auckland: Penguin, 2005).

Uren, Martyn, *Kiwi Saga: Memoirs of a New Zealand artilleryman* (Auckland: Collins, 1946).

——— *Diamond Trails of Italy* (Auckland: Collins, 1945).

Vaughan, Terry, *Whistle as You Go: The story of the Kiwi concert party and Terry Vaughan* (Auckland: Random House, 1995).

Wright, Matthew, *Freyberg: A life's journey* (Auckland: Oratia Books, 2020).

Unpublished archival sources

Charles James Watkins: Research papers relating to prisoner of war (Miscellaneous papers relating to prisoners of war), Alexander Turnbull Library, MS-Papers-8627-09.

A Sheffield Heritage: The Jones, Wilson & Related Families of Northern Tasmania & New Zealand, compiled by Rob Knight. Unpublished family history, n.d.

Papers Past — references to Jack Arnott (by date)

'Ringside Topics', *Evening Star*, issue 21565, 10 November 1933, https://paperspast.natlib.govt.nz/newspapers/ESD19331110.2.25.5

'Ringside Topics', *Evening Star*, issue 21623, 19 January 1934, https://paperspast.natlib.govt.nz/newspapers/ESD19340119.2.31.3

'Ringside Topics', *Evening Star*, issue 21629, 26 January 1934, https://paperspast.natlib.govt.nz/newspapers/ESD19340126.2.24.4

'Amateur Boxing', *Evening Star*, issue 21732, 29 May 1934, https://paperspast.natlib.govt.nz/newspapers/ESD19340529.2.114

'Boxing', *Evening Star*, issue 21826, 15 September 1934, https://paperspast.natlib.govt.nz/newspapers/ESD19340915.2.32.9

Evening Star, issue 21827, 17 September 1934, https://paperspast.natlib.govt.nz/newspapers/ESD19340917.2.28

'Topical tattle', *Evening Star*, issue 21911, 24 December 1934, https://paperspast.natlib.govt.nz/newspapers/ESD19341224.2.20

'Track and Field', *Evening Star*, issue 21937, 25 January 1935, https://paperspast.natlib.govt.nz/newspapers/ESD19350125.2.27.10

'Boxing Attraction', *Otago Daily Times*, issue 22910, 18 June 1936, https://paperspast.natlib.govt.nz/newspapers/ODT19360618.2.144

'Hughes-Stirling Fight', *Evening Star*, issue 22369, 19 June 1936; *Otago Daily Times*, issue 22912, 20 June 1936, https://paperspast.natlib.govt.nz/newspapers/ESD19360619.2.30

'Athletics', *Alexandra Herald and Central Otago Gazette*, issue 2070, 11 November 1936, https://paperspast.natlib.govt.nz/newspapers/AHCOG19361111.2.29

'Third Echelon: Improved Enlistments Yesterday', *Evening Star*, issue 23523, 12 March 1940, https://paperspast.natlib.govt.nz/newspapers/ESD19400312.2.57;

'Expeditionary Force', *Otago Daily Times*, issue 24246, 13 March 1940, https://paperspast.natlib.govt.nz/newspapers/ODT19400313.2.74

'Overseas Force', *Otago Daily Times*, issue 24297, 14 May 1940, https://paperspast.natlib.govt.nz/newspapers/ODT19400313.2.74

Evening Star, issue 24082, 31 December 1941, https://paperspast.natlib.govt.nz/newspapers/ESD19411231.2.20

Evening Star, issue 24116, 10 February 1942, https://paperspast.natlib.govt.nz/newspapers/ESD19420210.2.8

Otago Daily Times, issue 24837, 10 February 1942, https://paperspast.natlib.govt.nz/newspapers/ODT19420210.2.62

'Repatriated men', *Waikato Times*, issue 22572, 28 March 1945, https://paperspast.natlib.govt.nz/newspapers/WT19450328.2.3

'Free again', *Otago Daily Times*, issue 25828, 26 April 1945, https://paperspast.natlib.govt.nz/newspapers/ODT19450426.2.68

'Milton', *Otago Daily Times*, issue 25876, 21 June 1945, https://paperspast.natlib.govt.nz/newspapers/ODT19450621.2.111.3

'Personal', *Otago Daily Times*, issue 25914, 4 August 1945, https://paperspast.natlib.govt.nz/newspapers/ODT19450804.2.28.1

'Births', *Otago Daily Times*, issue 26233, 17 August 1946, https://paperspast.natlib.govt.nz/newspapers/ODT19460817.2.2.1

Further online resources

Carson, Terry, 'Papakura's 1940 Influenza Epidemic', Papakura Museum Blog, https://papakuramuseumblog.wordpress.com/2018/02/21/papakuras-1940-influenza-epidemic/

Cox, Peter. https://www.sidirezegh.co.nz/Operation-Crusader-An-Overview/

Fenton, Ken, 'Ken Fenton's War', https://kenfentonswar.com/stalag-357/

Green, Philip, 'WW2 People's War' (an online archive of wartime memories contributed by members of the public and gathered by the BBC), https://www.bbc.co.uk/history/ww2peopleswar/stories/34/a5248334.shtml

Grey, Paul and Sally, *Private J. D. Caves: The Long Journey Home*, Electronic Text Collection Te Pūhikotuhi o Aotearoa, Auckland, https://nzetc.victoria.ac.nz/tm/scholarly/tei-GreLong-t1-front-d5.html

https://www.anzacpow.com/part_1__missing_in_action,_believed_pow/chapter_5__italian_prison_camps

https://nzhistory.govt.nz/war/second-world-war/prisoners-of-war

https://nzhistory.govt.nz/war/second-world-war/prisoners-of-war/further-information

https://nzetc.victoria.ac.nz/tm/scholarly/tei-WH2Pris-_N84741.html

https://www.sidirezegh.co.nz/Operation-Crusader-An-Overview/

Liddle, Peter and Ian Whitehead, 'Not the Image but Reality: British POW Experiences In Italian and German Camps', https://war-experience.org/events/british-pow-experiences-in-italian-and-german-camps/

Ministry for Culture and Heritage, 'Daily life', https://nzhistory.govt.nz/war/second-world-war/prisoners-of-war/daily-life

Nominal Roll of NZ Escapees and Evaders — 1 New Zealand Interrogation Section Book 1, https://ndhadeliver.natlib.govt.nz/delivery/DeliveryManagerServlet?dps_pid=IE70135240

Quante storie: Campo 52: il campo di concentramento di Pian di Coreglia/So many stories: Campo 52: the concentration camp of Pian di Coreglia, www.raiplay.it/video/2020/01/campo-52-il-campo-di-concentramento-di-pian-di-coreglia--quante-storie-ed093e48-150f-4649-8758-fae2d3dd0e9f.html https://www.piazzalevante.it/2020/01/23/campo-52

Second World War Official Histories, Appendix 1 A. E. Field, Prisoners of the Germans and Italians, https://www.awm.gov.au/collection/C1417197

Auckland War Memorial Museum (AWMM) Tāmaki Paenga Hira (AWMM)

Second New Zealand Expeditionary Force, Nominal Roll Second New Zealand Expeditionary Force No. 3 (Embarkations from 1st July 1940 to 31st March 1941), (Wellington Government Printer: 1941), AWMM.

List of 2NZEF Prisoners of War, 1941–1945, Auckland War Memorial Museum Library, MS 2009/8, AWMM.

Great Britain Army, Germany and German Occupied Territories: Imperial prisoners of war alphabetical list: Section 4 (London: Government Printer: 1945), AWMM.

Great Britain Army, Italy: Imperial prisoners of war alphabetical list: Section 4 (London, Government Printer: 1945), AWMM.

Acknowledgements

When I gave up full-time employment in 2019, I finally had the impetus to apply for my father's army and medical records. However, it was only when my son casually revealed that he had a collection of ephemera, including photographs taken during Jack's internment, that I found the material that could help bring his war experiences to life. Ironically, these items had been sitting in his old tin army trunk in our loft, under a bag of punk records, only a couple of metres from where I work.

I make no pretence of being a military historian, and so any errors in the book are mine alone.

I am immensely grateful for the time and dedication given by those who have created records, written books, and collated websites that are accessible to all. In spite of having gleaned as much as I can from these archival sources, inevitably my text will contain gaps, longeurs, errors and false understandings, for which I apologise in advance.

We grew up thinking we weren't really Arnotts, and so I want to acknowledge my Arnott cousins, who have been so helpful in filling in gaps in my father's childhood. We rarely saw them during my childhood, but I am delighted to have got closer to them now. I would also like to thank the cousins with whom we spent time during the summers, and who stayed at 37 Landscape Road, for their valuable perspective.

I want to thank the Milton Facebook page for putting me in contact with Sue and Kevin Gorton, who were generous with their warmth and hospitality, to Keith Rogan, and my dear friend Scott for accompanying me on my journey south.

At Tāmaki Paenga Hira Auckland War Memorial Museum I am very grateful to Catherine Hammond and David Reeves in supporting my appointment as Research Associate, Documentary Heritage. Paula Legel is Associate Curator, Heritage Publications, who with assistance from the Stout Trust became my intrepid research companion in Italy. Her sensitivity and personal comprehension of what it is like to stand in the place where a loved one has suffered has been invaluable. I am particularly grateful to Didier Duja for that remarkable day in Friuli.

My warm thanks, as ever, go to John McIver, who patiently took Dad's tiny photographs and turned them into something publishable. I wish to acknowledge the librarians and archivists at: Alexander Turnbull Library, Wellington; Te Rua Mahara o te Kāwanatanga Archives New Zealand; Military History Library: Kippenberger Research Library, National Army Museum Te Mata Toa; Auckland Museum Tāmaki Paenga Hira; Auckland Library and Sir George Grey Special Collections; and Hocken Collections Uare Taoka o Hākena, Dunedin.

My personal thanks also go to Peter Cox, who kindly discovered my father's sporting records on *Papers Past*, and who generously allowed me to include the colour photograph of the mosque at Sidi Rezegh, where he made his own personal journey. I also recognise New Zealand expatriate artist and old friend, Susan Wilson, whose father became a stretcher bearer after the Battle of Monte Cassino.

Sue has close ties to the Monte San Martino Trust which was set up to acknowledge the bravery of the Italian country people who rescued many of the 50,000 Allied POWs on the run after the Armistice in September 1943.

I would also like to thank Nicola Legat and her team at Massey University Press for encouraging me to step into troubled waters, and Jane Parkin whose sage advice and sensitive editing were much appreciated.

I am deeply grateful to my son, who loved his grandad and kept his archive safe. Finally, I thank my husband, David Kisler. who having served in the British Army was able to fill in the gaps of my parlous military knowledge. He recognised the value in Dad, taking it on himself to provide invaluable research and writing on the highly confusing Battle of Sidi Rezegh. He not only did his utmost to clarify for me the vagaries of military structures and its arcane vocabulary, but also introduced me to the humour that lurks on the borders of day-to-day military life.

About the author

Art historian, curator and writer Mary Kisler MNZM worked for 21 years at Auckland Art Gallery Toi o Tāmaki, latterly as Senior Curator, Mackelvie Collection, International Art. In 2016, she was Craig Hugh Smyth Fellow at the Harvard Centre for Renaissance Art, Villa I Tatti, Florence, researching Italian works held in New Zealand Public Collections. Her previous publications include *Angels & Aristocrats: Early European art in New Zealand public collections* (Godwit, 2010); *Finding Frances Hodgkins* (Massey University Press, 2019), and, as contributing author and co-editor with Catherine Hammond, *Frances Hodgkins — European Journeys* (Auckland University Press in association with Auckland Art Gallery Toi o Tāmaki, 2019 and Thames and Hudson, 2019). Kisler also helped to create www.completefranceshodgkins.com.

First published in 2025 by Massey University Press
Private Bag 102904, North Shore Mail Centre
Auckland 0745, New Zealand
www.masseypress.ac.nz

Design by Carolyn Lewis
Cover photograph of Jack Arnott courtesy of the author
Back cover photograph of PG 66, Capua, courtesy of the International Committee of the Red Cross Audiovisual Archives

A catalogue record for this book is available from the National Library of New Zealand

Printed and bound in China by Everbest Investment Ltd

ISBN: 978-1-99-101656-0
eISBN: 978-1-99-101657-7

The assistance of Creative New Zealand is gratefully acknowledged by the publisher